MW01628254

VITA *Brevis*

Jill Medvedow and Carole Anne Meehan

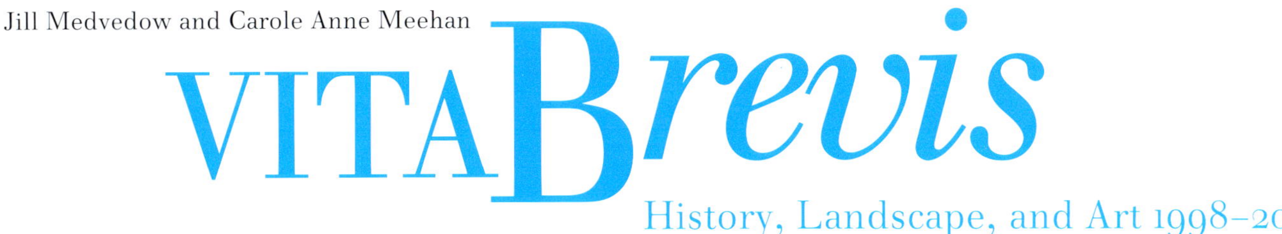

VITA Brevis

History, Landscape, and Art 1998–2003

with contributions by Jessica Morgan,
John Stilgoe, Paul Tucker,
and Emily Moore

ICA / STEIDL

Contents

Introduction by Jessica Morgan p. 7
Contours and Context: Five Years of Vita Brevis by Jill Medvedow p. 9
Vita Brevis in Tempore Contrario by Paul Tucker p. 17
Park Setting Time by John Stilgoe p. 23

Interviews with artists by Carole Anne Meehan

Let Freedom Ring
The Inaugural ICA/Vita Brevis Project
September 1998
- Jim Hodges, *Here We Are* p. 30
- Mildred Howard, *S.S.* p. 34
- Barbara Steinman, *Colonnade* p. 38
- Krzysztof Wodiczko, *Bunker Hill Monument Projection* p. 42

Shimon Attie: *An Unusually Bad Lot*
The 2nd Annual ICA/Vita Brevis Project
December 1999 p. 48

Art on the Emerald Necklace
The 3rd Annual ICA/Vita Brevis Project
Summer 2000
- James Boorstein, *Emanations* p. 54
- Ann Carlson, *Any Day Now* p. 58
- Ellen Driscoll, *Meanderlink* p. 62
- Barnaby Evans, *Moving Water* p. 66
- Sheila Kennedy, Frano Violich, *Common Pleasures: Parkway* p. 70
- Cornelia Parker, *At the Bottom of This Lake* p. 74
- Nari Ward, *Beautiful Necessity: Hugging Post* p. 78

Olafur Eliasson: *The young land*
The 4th Annual ICA/Vita Brevis Project
Summer 2001 p. 84

Ann Carlson and Mary Ellen Strom: *Remedy*
The 5th Annual ICA/Vita Brevis Project
May 2003 p. 90

Artists' Biographies by Emily Moore p. 96
Acknowledgements p. 101
ICA Trustees and Staff p. 102

Introduction by Jessica Morgan
Curator, Tate Modern

Returning from New York one summer evening in 1998, heading toward downtown Boston in a taxi from Logan Airport, my attention was caught by the brilliance of the Bunker Hill Monument in Charlestown, a familiar site, but this night transformed by light. The bluish illumination, I realized, was created by an enormous video projection of a female figure who appeared apparition-like at the top of the tower. She was speaking to me, or rather to anyone who happened to be looking at her, not performing as much as trying to convey something: a message or lecture, perhaps. Or was it some kind of live event? Clearly she was not a media personality or an actress in an advertisement: her appearance, gestures, and clothing were too mundane for that. Nor did she seem to have any religious or historical significance: there was nothing symbolic about her matronly, everyday look. So what justified her exalted position atop one of Greater Boston's most prominent landmarks? The view was soon eclipsed, leaving my curiosity unsatisfied. This turned out to be just one of a series of unexplained encounters in the city of Boston that summer.

Reluctantly revisiting the sites of the Freedom Trail with vacationing relatives a few days later, I was surprised to find evidence of incursions into these otherwise perhaps too-perfectly preserved historic sites. At the Old North Church, for example, a tree had been decorated with wind chimes. So many, in fact, that clearly this was not the casual work of a lone neighbor or passerby, but the effort of someone intending to draw attention, aurally, to this historic spot. The constant tinkling of the chimes was reminiscent of many cultures' use of bells or peals to mark significant stages of a ceremony, but the relentless ringing suggested some kind of gentle alarm or insistence on the presence of the location. The Old South Meeting House was similarly altered. A gilded train track ran through its austere interior, a literal translation, it seemed, of the Underground Railroad that enabled passage of so many slaves into freedom. Both projects, stumbled across unexpectedly, were more understandable than my far-off view of the Bunker Hill video, but I had the impression that some mysterious force at work in the city was determined to reanimate these over-determined sites.

Weeks later, reading an art review, I discovered that these were artworks organized as part of a series of projects under the auspices of Vita Brevis. The Bunker Hill project was by Krzysztof Wodiczko, a well-known public artist with an activist bent, who for this work had discussed with residents of Charlestown the numerous homicides in the area that had gone unresolved due to the silence of witnesses and potential informers. The figure I had seen was most likely the mother of one of the victims, her speech a declaration or plea for communication. Despite some disappointment about not having been able to hear her voice, this discovery made me think about the nature of public artworks. I considered the peculiarity of their unannounced, unexpected discovery and the manner in which our half understandings can lead to many possible interpretations. Rather than taking away from the intended meaning, these in fact begin to fulfill the communal ownership and collective interpretation that such public works seek to achieve. The mistake of the traditional monument, it seems, is always to assume a permanence and singularity of significance when the real potential of the public site is its changeability and flux.

The failure of the monument in recent years (with the exception of such oft-mentioned successes such as Maya Lin's Vietnam Memorial) made this series of Vita Brevis works particularly poignant. Just that summer Boston had erected a generally maligned statue dedicated to those who lost their lives in the Irish Famine. The bronze sculpture suffered from the all-too-graphic narrative and representational attributes that characterize the majority of public works. In a city where history looms so large, the sculpture's artistic treatment was lamentably lacking in subtlety and failed to question issues of authorship and representation. While academia had been pioneering the importance of recognizing differential reception, public artworks had blindly continued to assume the communal representation provided by the obligatory statue or plaque. Vita Brevis, it seemed, set about to manifest an "unworking" of community rather than its representation, to question who was being spoken for and which history was being told. This approach continued in the following year's Vita Brevis project by Shimon Attie, who chose to bring back to life the nineteenth-century stories and circumstances documented in the files of the now defunct police station that had once occupied the space of the ICA.

The confusion, or half-knowledge, that had pleasantly characterized my first encounters with these public projects ended in 1999 when I joined the staff at the museum and learned first-hand about the program's development. Now, however, I was able to enjoy others' confusion and the urban mythology that began to circulate during the subsequent projects. In the summer of 2000 I overheard teenagers in the Fenway telling each other that "part of the moon fell in this lake" (a result of Cornelia Parker's wonderfully poetic signs that documented the landing of the lunar meteorites she had thrown into the Fenway's water); watched the astonished reaction of visitors to Franklin Park who witnessed choreographer Ann Carlson's *tableau vivant* recreation of an early twentieth-century group's visit to a now abandoned zoo display; and, perhaps most enjoyable of all, observed the mental and spatial leaps evoked by Olafur Eliasson's *The young land*, a waterborne park of Icelandic lava rock that had mysteriously washed ashore on Boston's Fan Pier.

I envy those who stumble innocently across these works, their world upset for a moment, their sense of place and time disrupted, and, hopefully, their comfortable assumptions confused. This unmooring–whether of everyday experience or historical convictions–is the lasting consequence of the otherwise fleeting impression of Vita Brevis.

Contours and Context: Five Years of Vita Brevis

by Jill Medvedow
James Sachs Plaut Director,
Institute of Contemporary Art

Inspired and motivated by certain individuals, experiences, and goals, I founded Vita Brevis in 1997. Of particular importance was the experience of working with my friend, the late artist Juan Muñoz. Juan was an artist in residence at the Isabella Stewart Gardner Museum in Boston in 1994, immersed in the idiosyncrasies of that singular institution as the springboard for producing new works of art. Across the street from the Gardner Museum lies the Back Bay Fens, an urban wild designed by Frederick Law Olmsted as part of his Emerald Necklace. Directly facing the museum is a small, still pond. Despite having completed his residency project for the Gardner, Juan saw the pond as a potential site for a new work of art.

Juan submerged two stereo speakers in the murky water, suspended so that their rims barely broke the surface. The speakers energized the landscape with an air of expectation and dislocation. The possibility that sound would emerge from the speakers belied the fact that they floated disconnected in the water. Silence and still water created an uneasy, almost ominous atmosphere in an otherwise peaceful landscape. Like his images of open mouths drawn in oilstick on paper that were framed in the Gardner's gallery, the outdoor installation was permeated with a sense of stifled, even smothered, sound.

Inspired by Juan's vision, Vita Brevis was launched as an independent organization to produce artworks in unusual places: ponds and parks, historic sites, riverbanks, and abandoned buildings. It was established by following the lead of artists, was fortified by learning from the best practice in the field, and responded to the need to build audiences for art outside the mainstream museums. The potential of the landscape to serve as both catalyst and background for new works of art, while certainly not original, spoke to the overarching goal of Vita Brevis: to find innovative strategies to connect Boston audiences to contemporary art.

At the same time, other cities were also experimenting with temporary projects in public art, notably Art Angel in London and Creative Time in New York City. Among its many projects, including a radio broadcast with Muñoz, Art Angel produced a remarkable work with British artist Rachel Whiteread. *House*, completed in 1993, caused a local controversy in London's East End where Whiteread made a concrete cast of the interior of a condemned row house. In New York, Creative Time brought similar boldness to its endeavors. As early as 1976, it presented Red Grooms's *Ruckus Manhattan* downtown at 88 Pine Street and pioneered site-specific temporary art installations with Art on the Beach and, later, Art in the Anchorage. In South Carolina, Mary Jane Jacob curated *Places with a Past* as part of Charleston's Spoleto Festival and brought an exhibition practice rooted in the complexities of simultaneous urban locations to the field of public art. Each of these endeavors served as a model for Vita Brevis. Functioning outside the conventional museum world, they actively commissioned new works of art, designed flexible organizational structures for staffing and production, intersected with other cultural disciplines and diverse communities, and were democratic in their access and availability.

Boston had nothing like it. Steeped and invested in its history, the city's reputation for nurturing and launching contemporary artists diminished greatly since John Singer Sargent and James Whistler painted here almost a century ago. Overshadowed by New York and other centers of contemporary art in the twentieth century, Bostonians flocked to exhibitions of Impressionist and early-twentieth-century art while exhibitions of post-war abstract expressionists, minimalists, pop artists, and conceptual artists were viewed only by a select few. Contemporary art in Boston remained overshadowed by historic sites and a long attachment to a more adventurous past, despite efforts by the Institute of Contemporary Art, which consistently presented adventurous international contemporary art since 1936, and subsequently by the university-based museums and galleries.

Vita Brevis began, in part, as an effort to identify broad ideas that already mattered to the local citizenry and use them as a bridge between audiences and art and artists. It proposed capitalizing on a strong identification with the city and replacing an innate disinterest in and disinclination toward contemporary art with proximity and familiarity.

The history and landscape of Boston became the basis for the new organization. Artists were invited to respond to these two arenas of cultural and natural wealth that Bostonians embraced with affection and knowledge, and they did so in ways that ranged from the poetic to the polemic. The work created during the first five years of Vita Brevis that is the subject of this publication falls into three broad categories reflective of the original premise: monument and memory; landscape and history; and contemporary heroism.

Many of the artists–Krzysztof Wodiczko, Barbara Steinman, Mildred Howard, and Shimon Attie, most specifically–wrought powerful reinterpretations of historic sites and memorials. The pervasive use of public and permanent monuments to commemorate acts of heroism and martyrdom is a timely and tense subject. The controversies surrounding the World Trade Center memorial raise crucial questions about public history and its authors and artists, much as they surrounded the creation of a national Holocaust Memorial in Berlin almost a decade ago. Commenting on artist Horst Hoheisel's radical proposal for the Berlin Memorial to destroy the landmark Brandenburger Tor, grind it into dust and scatter the remains over the vanished site, historian James Young suggests eloquently that perhaps "only an unfinished memorial process can guarantee the life of memory." [1] Permanent monuments, from traditional statuary to more recent installations, such as that commemorating the Oklahoma City deaths by artists Hans and Torrey Butzer and Sven Berg, and the most recent competition in New York City for the World Trade Center site are fixed statements of loss and the collective memory of loss, and are usually accompanied by extensive community process, bargaining, and municipal or national politics. The idea suggested by James Young that memory may be best served by absence or an evolving process helped to define the temporary nature of Vita Brevis.

Boston, too, has an abundance of sites marking loss from the Revolutionary and Civil Wars. The military and political battles commemorated by places such as the Old South Meeting House, Bunker Hill Monument, Underground Railroad stops, and Faneuil Hall resonate with large themes in American life. The visual reinterpretation of freedom and democracy in Vita Brevis artworks linked the earlier historical eras with personal perspectives and current social struggles.

James Boorstein, Ellen Driscoll, Jim Hodges, Cornelia Parker, Barnaby Evans, Sheila Kennedy and Frano Violich, and Olafur Eliasson responded more directly to the shaped or naturally formed landscape either through intervention or framing. Unlike the fixed facades of granite, marble, and brick monuments, these artists approached their projects fully aware of the continuously changing nature of the landscape. From the outset, they demonstrated an awareness of the life cycle of Frederick Law Olmsted's system of linked parks and its corresponding evolution, erosion, decay, replanting, and passive and active neglect. The neighborhoods abutting the parks have also changed in the more than one hundred years since Olmsted's work, and many of the works reflected those changes.

Finally, and in direct response to the altered world post September 11, 2001, Ann Carlson, in collaboration with Mary Ellen Strom, used movement and videography to focus on personal heroism and to reveal the daily acts of humanity often unseen in the institutions of medicine and public health. Carlson took Vita Brevis in a new direction, one that centered on individual behavior, absent of a historical or environmental setting. Working to define the medical and cultural communities as stewards of physical and spiritual health, Carlson used the processes of public art to forge new connections in Boston.

Vita Brevis took its name from the Latin adage *Ars Longa, Vita Brevis*, Art is long, life is brief. While the works were always intended to be temporary in nature, the name summed up the urgency to find long-term artistic solutions to a shrinking public culture. Graphic designer Lorraine Wild was hired to find a visual expression for the nascent organization. Now in the permanent collection of the San Francisco Museum of Modern Art, Wild's graphics for Vita Brevis brilliantly captured the transitory yet grounded ideas of the endeavor. In 1998, with an identity and an initial project underway, ICA/Vita Brevis became a permanent program of the Institute of Contemporary Art. The stage was set for its inaugural presentation.

I. *Let Freedom Ring*

Vita Brevis presented its first public project in 1998 using Boston's Freedom Trail as its organizing principle and its location and thus taking on some of the most revered and popular historic sites in the city. In *Let Freedom Ring*, artists Jim Hodges, Mildred Howard, Barbara Steinman, and Krzysztof Wodiczko selected the Bigelow Courtyard behind the Old North Church, the Old South Meeting House, the Parkman Bandstand on the Boston Common, and the Bunker Hill Monument for their projects. Historian Marilyn Richardson's essay on the project was a reminder that while visitors brought to "each of these sites a private mix of factoids recalled from history books or school field trips," they were ultimately "invited to think about those ancient protagonists Freedom and Tyranny and the many ways they have duked it out over the centuries here on our home turf."[2]

Each project implicitly or overtly referred to known historical persons or periods. Mildred Howard evoked the arduous journey of fugitive slaves traveling north via the Underground Railroad. Siting her piece in the sanctuary of the Old South Meeting House, where colonial Bostonians came to worship, rally, protest, celebrate, and convene, Howard's work, entitled *S.S.*, explored congregation and movement. Consisting of railroad tracks and ties running through the sanctuary toward a tabletop of cannonballs, Howard's piece was a reminder of Frederick Douglass's insight that "without struggle, there can be no progress." As viewers walked down the tracks around a corner toward the piece's conclusion, a backwards glance caught one's reflection in a gold-leafed mirror, a poignant reminder that freedom is a living idea.

Jim Hodges gathered hundreds of windchimes from all around the country and strung them from the treetops in the enclosed Bigelow Courtyard adjacent to the Old North Church in Boston's North End. Famous for its steeple where, in 1775, sexton Robert Newman hung the two lanterns immortalized in "one if by land, two if by sea," Old North Church continues to be an active Episcopal congregation. Hodges's piece, entitled *Here We Are*, echoed the visual memory of lanterns signaling a call to revolutionary action with the elusive sound of wind chimes. "The chimes are spirits, memories called forth from an historic site, the voices of the missing," said Hodges at the time. The artist composed a short poem for a wooden plaque placed at the entry to the courtyard:

> Here we are
> At this place between places
> A great historic monument
> Ourselves

His sound piece, like Howard's installation, was a potent representation of democracy as accessible and diverse. It invoked the quiet power of individual memory and responsibility.

Barbara Steinman tackled the weight and meaning of collective memory in her work, *Colonnade*, at the Parkman Bandstand on the Boston Common. Purchased in 1634 by the Puritans of the Massachusetts Bay Colony for use as a common area for sheep and cow grazing, military exercises, and public executions, the Common today is a tree-lined park filled with human activities and innumerable historical monuments and plaques. With few exceptions, the memorials commemorate the deaths of men from war. Solid and sculptural, they employ beautiful stones, turns of phrase, typefaces and engravings to achieve their permanence and immutability.

Steinman stealthily photographed and traced the faces of the plaques, collecting and rearranging the chiseled words into new phrases, and transferred them onto 12-foot-high banners that hung vertically from the twelve Ionic columns of the graceful Bandstand. A detail picturing a wing from the Boston Massacre appeared on the exterior of each of the cloth panels. Together the manipulated words and images billowed in the changing wind on the Common, dramatically altering both the original meaning of the plaques and the solid appearance of the Bandstand. In the place of monuments to men, war, and permanence, Barbara Steinman used the rounded and feminine structure of the Parkman Bandstand to create an ephemeral poem of hope and freedom.

Unlike the first three projects, which were intended to be part of a walking tour and open for an extended period of time, Krzysztof Wodiczko's *Bunker Hill Monument Projection* was on view for only three nights. After many months of interaction with residents of Charlestown, where the Bunker Hill Monument is located, Wodiczko chose as his subject the high number of unsolved deaths of young men in Charlestown that has plagued this area for almost twenty years. Three quarters of those deaths, from homicide, suicide, and drugs, remained unsolved because of a "code of silence," leaving a legacy of pain and grieving.

The towering Bunker Hill Monument was built as a memorial to young men of an earlier era. Dedicated in 1843, it commemorates the battle between colonial and British troops on Charlestown's Breed's Hill. The confrontation was won by the British, but, despite the loss, the fortitude of the American patriots to resist the British forces led the colonies to form their own army, formalizing the launch of the Revolutionary War. Interestingly, in 1840, when the Bunker Hill Monument Association ran out of funds to complete the monument, it was salvaged by a Ladies' Fair at Boston's Quincy Market that sold crafts, food, and books and raised the final $30,000 necessary to finish the job.[3]

One hundred and fifty five years later, Krzysztof Wodiczko recognized the heroism of a different group of women whose lives intersected with the Bunker Hill Monument. For three nights running, Wodiczko projected the faces, hands and voices of five Charlestown residents–three mothers and two brothers–whose lives had been devastated by the deaths of their children and siblings. Each evening, Sandy King, Terry Titcomb, Pam Enos, Steven Kozlowski, and Michael Patrick MacDonald told their stories from the top of the Monument, transforming the solid, 221- foot-high Egyptian-style obelisk into what critic Ken Shulman called "a nighttime granite goddess, its massive form made weightless through animation and then weighty with the gravity of these mothers' tales."[4]

The 19-minute projection was chilling and magnificent, drawing together residents of Charlestown and the Greater Boston community. While acclaimed by the critics and the general public, some residents of Charlestown were disturbed by the work and the public disclosure of community pain. Like the film *Monument Ave.*, which coincidentally premiered in Boston the same weekend and also depicted the drugs and gangs of Charlestown, as well the more recent *Mystic River*, the Monument Projection exposed the conflicts of a changing, rapidly gentrifying neighborhood as well as the dark underside of cyclical poverty and underemployment.

Even more, the *Projection* challenged the sacred premises of the Monument by equating the national loss of life and sacrifice of the men in the Revolutionary War with the local loss of life and sacrifice of the men and women of present-day Charlestown. It was seen as sacrilege by some, a brilliant reinterpretation of public history by others. By projecting the pain of mothers on the archtypical male structure of the obelisk, Krzysztof Wodiczko feminized, elevated, and infused the Bunker Hill Monument with new meaning, enabling it, in the artist's words, to assert its First Amendment rights to speak about what it had witnessed.

Let Freedom Ring, the inaugural Vita Brevis project, raised a chorus of previously silenced voices. Mildred Howard evoked those of runaway slaves. Krzysztof Wodiczko amplified the words of grieving mothers. Barbara Steinman feminized the voices of the Revolutionary and Civil Wars. Jim Hodges quietly conveyed the whispering sounds of loved ones through the music of his chimes. The artists' reuse and reinterpretation of historic places and monuments added new voices and layers of meaning, challenging the long-held view that that "history is written by the victors." They transformed the memorials, once fixed in time and material, to reflect a more complex and evolutionary sense of history.

II. *An Unusually Bad Lot*

Shimon Attie also worked in the contested arena of public space and public memory. Selecting as his site the façade of the ICA's building at 955 Boylston Street in the Back Bay neighborhood, Attie's fascination was with the histories contained within the building, a former police station, rather than with the monumentality and symbolism of the architecture. The Division 16 Police Station, built in 1885 in the style of H. H. Richardson, served as a holding station for prisoners and the division headquarters for seventy-nine years.

As in his public pieces in Berlin, Copenhagen, and New York, Attie employed the artistic materials and techniques of light and composition to connect historical architecture and actions with current psychological and political states. Like *Writing on the Wall*, where he projected slide images of Jewish storefronts in Berlin destroyed and erased during WWII onto their former locations, Attie delved into the written and photographic documents from the police archives and used them as the source materials of his art.

An Unusually Bad Lot, the 2nd Annual ICA/Vita Brevis Project, used lasers and slide projections to transform the ICA façade into a living archive and reveal turn of the century attitudes about criminality and deviancy. Journal entries from arresting policemen, judges, and social workers exposed the prejudices about class, race, and sexuality that biased arrests in the late nineteenth century. Attie scrolled cursive writing up and down the walls of the building, spelling out quotes and citations such as, "She did not seem to feel ashamed being arrested for fornication, not even with a colored man," and "he is something of a verbalist and has a reputation as a homosexualist."

By projecting images of mug shots and using the lasers to write out file notes, Attie employed the temporal qualities of light to fill the gap between the past and the present. Haunting and ghostlike, the images and text appeared and vanished on the solid face of the building, and contrasted the "ambiguous relation between absence and presence, between physicality and ephemerality."[5] In *An Unusually Bad Lot*, Attie resurrected not just the images, but the memory of their presence into the present moment.

III. *Art on the Emerald Necklace*

Unlike the reinterpretations of the historic monument, memory, and the memorial during the first two years of Vita Brevis, artists James Boorstein, Ann Carlson, Ellen Driscoll, Barnaby Evans, Sheila Kennedy and Frano Violich, Cornelia Parker, and Nari Ward responded more directly to the physical landscape of Boston. In *Art on the Emerald Necklace*, presented in the summer of 2000 as the 3rd Annual ICA/Vita Brevis Project, these artists were invited to respond to the places, ideas, or sites of Frederick Law Olmsted's Emerald Necklace, the meandering series of nine parks and green spaces he designed in the late 1800s. The Emerald Necklace exemplified Olmsted's democratic, if not downright utopian, belief in the ability of public parks to promote health, democracy, and communication. Olmsted envisioned the parks as places where people from different classes could come together and find respite from the crowded, unsanitary conditions of city life. The aesthetic conventions and techniques he used were employed to achieve these goals. As critic Ann Wilson Lloyd observed, "Olmsted's designs were planned to engineer how people moved through them, with wide malls in which to gather, meandering pathways that encouraged contemplation of picturesque, natural-looking (but often highly manufactured) vistas, and interlacing carriage trails, bridged or sunken so as not to interrupt the leisurely pace of strollers." [6]

This combination of landscape and social history, public sites and hidden treasures, ways of seeing and moving through space, and ideas about natural and manufactured beauty, were fertile ground for the eight artists in *Art on the Emerald Necklace*. With few exceptions, most of the artists consciously made a minimalist intervention into the landscape. Unlike the artists in the 1960s and '70s, such as Michael Heizer, Dennis Oppenheim, and Robert Morris, who created minimalist forms in their earthworks but brought a Western ruggedness and bravado to achieve a monumentality of experience, the artists participating in the Emerald Necklace project brought an almost deferential attitude toward Olmsted. Yet, in their concept and appearance, most of the projects echoed the land art/earthworks of the earlier decades much more than what has come to define the public art of the '90s and current moment.

James Boorstein selected Ward's Pond as the site for his piece, *Emanations*. Secluded and serene, Ward's Pond, frequented mainly by dog walkers and fishermen, is a surprising refuge just minutes from a major road. In *Emanations*, Boorstein mechanically created a series of concentric ripples on the pond's surface, giving the illusion of stones tossed into the water. To see the piece, viewers had to leave the beaten path and walk to the water's edge. With the intermittent disruption of the water, visitors begin to notice the small details of the overgrown site: its turtles, fish, and birds, a small path skirting along the perimeter, the dense and varied foliage. *Emanations* had echoes of a Japanese garden where the ripples in the sand are repeated in the water, using the abstraction of the external structure to invite inward focus and attention.

In her book *Overlay*, author Lucy Lippard notes that "certain forms have survived the (intervening) millennia as the vehicles for such a vital expression. The concentric circle; the spiral, the meander, the zigzag, the lozenge or diamond shape, the line in the landscape, the passage and labyrinth and welcome, terrifying shelter are still meaningful to us, even if we cannot cite their sources and symbolic intricacies. These forms seem to have some basic connection to human identity, confirming bonds we have almost lost with the land, its products and its cycles, and with each other."[7] These natural forms found expression in Boorstein's *Emanations*, as they did in Olmsted's designs. The images in both of their work, each requiring the technologies of their time, mirrored the movement of waves and rivers and, in their use of abstract, archtypical forms, evoked the simplicity and profundity of the pre-modern landscape.

Cornelia Parker also chose the water's edge for her work, *At the Bottom of This Lake*. At Leverett Pond and the Back Bay Fens Lagoon, Parker privately dropped into these bodies of water two meteorite fragments, purchased by the artist on e-bay. She then marked the events with cast-iron plaques. "At the Bottom of This Lake Lies a Fragment of a Star," read one. The signage not only marked the site but it framed a very specific view across the water and created a mythological narrative of a falling star. Like much of Parker's work, this piece involved the witty transformation of an ominous threat of a meteoric fireball into a small, harmless rock tossed by hand into the water. In the process, however, the possibility that a piece of the sky may have fallen to earth is sparked, causing passersby to note the event and record it in their own version of geologic history, or even to read it as an omen of things to come. As Jessica Morgan points out, Parker's light touch with the meteor is a knowing "riposte to the elaborate machismo of '60s and '70s earthworks artists. While Michael Heizer's *Double Negative* may have required the complicated removal of many tons of earth and Walter de Maria's *Lightning Field* required similarly massive production, Parker had brought about a celestial counterpart to the earthworks while creating no more than a ripple of water."[8]

Ellen Driscoll hovered at an altogether different edge, bringing Olmsted's notion of peripheral vision to new heights in her work, *Meanderlink*. Olmsted believed that what is seen out of the corners of the eye or above it is as vital to the imagination as looking straight ahead or down at the ground, as is much more common. Driscoll took the skies as her location, and in an effort to encourage people to look up, flew banners of her own design from the back of small planes. Typically a site for advertising, like the Goodyear blimp or ballgame media, Driscoll's design was a graphic depiction of the park system looking like spider webs, or cellular structures, organic and associative in their appearance.

Where Boorstein, Driscoll, and Parker celebrated and "remythologized" Olmsted's work, collaborative artists and architects Sheila Kennedy and Frano Violich chose a decidedly unattractive and neglected aspect of the Necklace for their site. The Monsignor William Casey Overpass connects Harvard University's Arnold Arboretum and the city's Franklin Park. Originally intended by Olmsted to be a tree-lined parkway, it is now a cement eyesore with neither space nor scenery for pedestrians. Kennedy and Violich attempted to fill in this missing "link" in the Necklace with links of their own. Attracted by the southern exposure, the public scale, and the long vistas of Boston, they installed panels of chain link fence vertically along the overpass in a work entitled *Common Pleasures: Parkway*. At the base of the fencing were pots of soil and starter plants of beans, tomatoes, and nasturtiums. Watered and tended by a group of neighborhood volunteers, the vertical garden beds were designed as a contemporary solution to reconnect this roadway to the Arboretum and the Park. Unfortunately and unpredictably, during a storm with unusually high wind, the work was damaged and had to be removed before the vegetables and flowers fully enveloped the fencing units.

Barnaby Evans also focused attention on a changed aspect of the Emerald Necklace and the environmental impact of that change. In *Moving Water*, Evans literally transported 147,000 gallons of water in a convoy of stainless-steel trucks from the Charles to the Muddy River to visually emphasize their connection. Olmsted offered a civil engineering solution to the problem of the polluted Muddy River and through excavations and landfill used the water of the Charles to sanitize that of the Muddy. After the Charles was dammed in 1910, the Muddy again descended into a stagnant body of water. On three consecutive Saturdays, Evans literally reconnected the two rivers by physically and publicly moving water from one to the other.

Like Kennedy and Violich, Ann Carlson and Nari Ward chose a spot of urban blight. Ward and Carlson were both attracted to a neglected corner of Franklin Park, at the far end of the Emerald Necklace. In the nineteenth century, Olmsted's design for this park included a Victorian zoo, with caged animals dispersed in different areas, unlike the contained zoos of our era. Still evident, though in disrepair, are several abandoned bear cages. Surrounded by lower-income and poor neighborhoods, the Playstead area of Franklin Park is not frequented by the typical participants in Boston's predominantly white art world. In fact, for many residents of Boston, it is psychologically off limits. Siting two works there was a challenging opportunity for discovery.

For her work, Carlson created a *tableau vivant* based on a 1915 archival photograph of a group of Victorian men and women leaning, in their leisure, on the iron railing, looking at the bears. In *Any Day Now*, period costumed dancers moved in slow, almost invisible, motion, from the park's popular playing field to the Playstead site. Taking a full two hours to cover ground that would normally require ten minutes, Carlson layered different kinds of time–historic, recreational, deliberate–as her dancers painstakingly moved through the activities of others. Leaving the open field, the dancers made their way to the denser growth of a deserted footpath, up crumbling cement steps to the Playstead. There, they arranged themselves into the exact positions of the photograph, transporting the audience literally and figuratively, one hundred years back in time.

Nari Ward, at the same Playstead site, made an imposing sculpture from a rusted metal cylindrical cage originally placed around trees to prevent the bears from climbing out of their confines. Ward relocated the 19-foot-high cage in front of the abandoned bear display. He raised it off the ground on stilts, surrounded it with carefully tended flower beds, and opened its door to the public. Titled *Beautiful Necessity: Hugging Post*, Ward's piece offered the opportunity to enter the cage and have an unusual perspective. Through the bars, the former bear enclosure is in plain view, as is the Seal of the City of Boston surrounded by two cast-concrete bears. In the bars, the perspective is of animal and human confinement and the power relationships that define such confinement. The idea Ward suggests in his *Hugging Post* subtitle adds a final postscript on the possibility of a more positive connection. In a project characterized by so many light touches and delicate interventions into the landscape, Ward's work also had the distinction of being the most materially substantial and accessible.

IV *The young land*

The 4th Annual ICA/Vita Brevis Project was not layered onto or inserted into the existing landscape. Rather it involved the creation of an entirely new land formation. In *The young land*, artist Olafur Eliasson floated twenty-two tons of lava on a barge in Boston Harbor. Sited directly off the shore below an imposing United States courthouse, the lava formed the ground of a floating park of small and large rocks. Viewers were invited to cross a small gangway onto the barge and experience the rolling waves, walk over the field of black rocks and watch as they revealed a multitude of colors and shapes. The unfamiliarity of the materials was enhanced by the disorienting perspective of standing offshore.

The title referred to the age of the volcanic rocks, which were brought from an inactive volcano in the artist's native Iceland. The 200-year-old rocks are geologically young compared with the stones and outcrops of the New England landscape, challenging our perspective about age and place in the physical universe.

In *The young land*, Eliasson repeatedly shifted the continuum between land and sea, imbalance and stability, and geologic time and human temporality. The floating bridge made a visual connection between the ocean and the land. Eliasson echoed the instability of the volcano with the precariousness of the barge. He mirrored the creation of the volcanic landscape with his own creation of a new, and young, addition to the Boston waterfront.

Immediately after the horrific attacks of September 11, 2001, *The young land* was abruptly removed while U.S. Federal Marshals held the ICA's tugboat operator at gunpoint from its courthouse site. The barge was returned to its owner and the twenty-two tons of lava were sent to storage for future use by the artist. With its long view of the history of the earth, its emphasis on shifting human perspectives, and encountering unfamiliar turf, Olafur Eliasson's *The young land* was a prescient, if brief, metaphor for a post 9/11 world.

V *Remedy*

Remedy by choreographer Ann Carlson, in collaboration with video artist Mary Ellen Strom, was, by contrast, directly affected by the events and aftermath of September 11, 2001. Like her earlier piece for Vita Brevis, *Remedy* was performance-based and involved many people in its presentation. In the development of *Remedy*, however, Carlson also involved numerous individuals whose professional lives formed the basis of the work. For eighteen months, Carlson interviewed and shadowed individuals directly involved in healing bodies and souls in Boston. She met repeatedly with public health officials to better understand the nature of public wellness, illness, and safety, and met with doctors, nurses, and staff at Children's Hospital to delve into their daily work lives. Ultimately, *Remedy* focused on the quotidian routines and movements of several hospital employees to reveal how physical mannerisms, small gestures, and identifiable patterns of movement could reveal the potency and power of individual efforts to heal.

Based on the idiosyncrasies of each participant, Carlson choreographed a series of individual movements, creating a short, unique dance. The intent of each dance was both external and internal, as a means of public communication with an audience, and as a point of inner focus and discipline for the dancer. At the conclusion of research, choreography and rehearsal, each dance was performed on stage at Children's Hospital for videotaping by Strom. The edited portraits were brought to the public on billboard-size LED screens which sat on the back of a flatbed truck that was driven to different locations in the city.

Carlson broke away from the structure of history and landscape that provided the context for all the previous Vita Brevis projects. Yet in her creation of individual portraits, she, too, asked the question of who defines patriotism. Like Barbara Steinman, Jim Hodges, Krzysztof Wodiczko, and Shimon Attie, Ann Carlson elevated the lives and livelihood of heroes and heroines whose names are otherwise unwritten or untold.

VI *Looking Forward*

The partners critical to the successful realization of Vita Brevis have been predominantly local, state, and federal agencies, neighborhood groups, local and national businesses and vendors, churches, historical sites and hospitals. Working with non-arts organizations as active collaborators required forging a shared vision of a city whose culture and public discourse would be enriched by increasing the relevance and use of public parks and historic sites and strengthened by a contemporary interpretation of Boston's past.

Although some of the Vita Brevis projects are presented for several hours while others for several months, each one is, in its essence, a brief moment in the historical and natural landscape of the city. The decision to steer clear of permanent memorials and focus on short-lived interventions frees the artists and the ICA from the many processes of consensus mandated by so many permanent public artworks and allows for a clear artistic vision to emerge. It also allows for many important questions about the permanent and transitory nature of art, nature, history, and memory to be raised. How does history stay alive? Are the idealistic goals that motivated the creation of public parks and urban design still relevant today? How does geologic time affect our understanding of progress? And, who are the guardians of health and healing?

The first five years of ICA/Vita Brevis have witnessed enormous transformations in the city and in the world, and each of the artists responded to the past and the future with insight and sensitivity about the evolutionary and changing nature of life and land. For Vita Brevis, the next five years holds the promise of equally provocative new works of art that grapple with history, landscape, and individual lives. Jennifer Allora, Guillermo Callzadilla, Ellen Band, and Julian Opie will create projects in Boston, and the Harbor Islands, much like the Emerald Necklace, will be the site for a major exhibition of new works in 2007.

In 1997 Vita Brevis was founded on the premise that it is vital, healing, and urgent to bring the creative process, and the contemporary work that results from it, back into the fabric of urban life. Six years later, fifteen artists received commissions and fourteen new works of art were created. Artworks were temporarily sited in numerous locations and in diverse neighborhoods, and over 500,000 people experienced the individual and shared pleasures provided by infusing time-honored places with the vision and contemporary perspective of today's exemplary artists.

Dedicated to Richard Kazis, Barbara Lee, Justine Liff, and Juan Muñoz.

1 James E. Young, *At Memory's Edge: After-Images of the Holocaust in Contemporary Art and Architecture*, New Haven and London: Yale University Press, 2000, p. 92.
2 Marilyn Richardson, essay written for the ICA's *Let Freedom Ring* handout, September 1998.
3 Sarah J. Purcell, "Commemoration, Public Art, and the Changing Meaning of the Bunker Hill Monument," *Public Historian*, vol. 25, no. 2, Spring 2003. (Purcell refers to Charles W. Snell, *Documents Relating to the Organization and Purpose of the Bunker Hill Monument Association and to the Construction of the Bunker Hill Monument, 1823–1846*, vol. II, Denver: National Park Service, United States Department of the Interior, 1982, p.128.
4 Ken Shulman, "A Monument to Mothers and Lost Children," *New York Times*, September 20, 1998, p. 40.
5 Norman L. Kleeblatt, "Persistence of Memory," *Art in America*, June 2000, p. 103.
6 Ann Wilson Lloyd, "Remembering Olmsted's Vision for Boston," *New York Times*, August 6, 2000, p. 33.
7 Lucy Lippard, *Overlay*, New York: Pantheon Books, 1983, pp. 10–11.
8 Jessica Morgan, "Meteor or Metaphor," *Cornelia Parker: a meteorite lands*, Ikon Gallery, 2002, p. 17

Vita Brevis in *Tempore Contrario*

by Paul Tucker
Professor of Art History, University of Massachusetts

These are curious, contradictory times in America, at once fickle and predictable, fleeting and extended. They give *vita brevis* a much sharper edge than the phrase possessed six years ago when Jill Medvedow adopted it for the temporary art projects she initiated in Boston and which the ICA has carried on so successfully under the astute direction of Carole Anne Meehan. Everything now seems to be alternately deeply significant or utterly irrelevant, surprisingly laden or emotionally vacuous. Confidence has been similarly bifurcated, emerging in some quarters with almost revolting excess, retreating in others with an equally abhorrent, cowardly haste. Not surprisingly, meaning–in the most general sense of the word–has been seriously challenged, if not victimized, causing it to vacillate between the insistent and the illusionary, the desired and the demeaned.

Evidence of the spasmodic state of affairs in the United States abounds in the arenas of politics and the economy–the logical loci for such strains, but it is also painfully apparent elsewhere–in the contrast between such mundane phenomena as the emergence of reality television programs or our increased obsession with Hollywood stars and the advances of undeniable importance that have occurred since the *Vita Brevis* project began–the successful mapping of the genome, for instance, or the discovery of an organism (in Mono Lake, California) comprised of genes that can exist in extreme conditions, such as those in outer space, raising the possibility of life elsewhere in our universe. Virtually everywhere one looks it seems there are baffling dichotomies–the rise of obesity in the U.S. and the concurrent explosion of fitness centers, or the startling knowledge gaps in the general populace and the surge of high school students scoring between 750 and 800 on their college boards. Given the power this country presently wields in the world, it is also perhaps surprising to learn that only 18–20% of the 290 million people who live in the United States hold active passports.[1]

Divisions of all kinds, of course, even extreme ones, have always characterized this country, as the U.S. has openly welcomed differences and conscientiously struggled to resolve them. We have also experienced many tumultuous periods in our past. The strain of our moment is, therefore, neither isolated nor unparalleled, but, unlike most others, it feels less the product of specific historical forces–the Vietnam War in the 1960s, for example, or Black Thursday of 1929–than the collision of intangible, internal contradictions that have arisen in the last few years with less warning and coordination, which makes them appear to be more pervasive and insidious.

These dichotomies–evident also in the arts as we shall see–are increasingly the subject of analysis by observers of the contemporary scene, most of whom underscore the late Edward

Said's assertion that the U.S. is "undergoing a serious clash of identities similar to other contests in the rest of the world." The 135 candidates who ran for the California governorship in the 2003 recall election is an absurd, though tangible, case in point.[2]

If we truly are in a semi-schizophrenic time, how can we account for it? Does it have something to do with the fundamental socio-economic reality that governs the U.S.: namely that while we live in the wealthiest nation in the world with one of the highest standards of living, many citizens do not enjoy the country's enviable advantages, a fact that derives from another undeniable reality–that the nation's collective wealth is controlled by a small minority? Economic chasms have always existed, although the divisions between classes have notably increased. In 1999, for example, the *New York Times* reported that the richest one percent of the U.S. population, 2.7 million people, had "as many after-tax dollars to spend as the bottom 100 million."[3]

Financial disparities are not the only cause of the problem, however. They may even be peripheral, as the U.S. remains relatively unique, in the Western world at least, for its unabashed belief in opportunity, and for its capacity to produce a seemingly continuous stream of real-life Horatio Alger stories generation after generation. Certain playing fields, therefore, have actually been leveled, including ones in the arts that we will turn to in a moment. Consider physical mobility. In Boston, it is less expensive to take a bus to New York City than a taxi to Logan Airport, though the latter is only a few miles away while New York lies nearly two hundred to the southeast. Private transportation has likewise expanded exponentially as more Americans are driving more vehicles than ever before. And they are driving them farther. In 1970, we covered slightly more than one trillion miles; in 2000 that number rose to nearly three trillion.[4]

Not coincidentally, the physical mobility that more Americans enjoy parallels the increased access they have to information today, obtained from a heretofore inconceivable array of options. So rapid and extensive has the development of mass communications been in the last decade in this country (as well as elsewhere in the world) that we tend to forget that the personal computer is only twenty years old, cable television is even younger, and satellite television newer still. In addition, most hand-held electric devices did not exist in the 1980s and were only used by a small percentage of the population in the early 1990s. Now they are everywhere.

Sociologists and specialists in communications theory have just begun to examine the ubiquity of the cell phone and the behavior it encourages.[5] But one conclusion is clear even to the untrained observer, namely that the cell phone breaks down barriers between public and private spaces, a phenomenon that is also at the heart of reality television programs and talk shows such as those hosted by Jerry Springer and Jenny Jones. This collapse, or merger, of the public and the private has a number of consequences, not the least of which is the way it legitimizes formerly despised, invasive practices like voyeurism and eavesdropping. Then, there are the false pretenses that such a collapse promotes. Among those is the way the base and ordinary are endowed with the aura of the significant, making anything and everything appear to be interesting, legitimate, important, and immediate.

The shallowness of such illusions, coupled with this unprecedented fusing of the public and the private, raises an array of serious questions, particularly about cultural production. How do we tell the good from the bad? Is there any point in making such judgments? By whose system are they made? What content or activity is worth our attention, who makes those decisions, and on what basis? And what are the consequences of those decisions?

All of this has direct bearing on the world of the arts, especially on work that receives public support or is destined for a public space. It could be argued, in fact, that public art has become *the* locus for the dichotomous conditions of our times, provoking contentious debate about the appropriate use of taxpayers' dollars as well as intense controversy about the relative merits of the specific project. So common have the battles about government funding of the arts been since the Robert Mapplethorpe debacle of the 1980s that one might also say it is almost un-American *not* to have an opinion about the benefits of a government-sponsored project.

Dissent about public art is not new. It actually began with one of the earliest pieces of public sculpture the federal government commissioned for the youthful republic–a statue of George Washington–a prize awarded in 1832 to a little-known sculptor from Boston, Horatio Greenough.[6] When the over-life-size, semi-nude figure of Washington was unveiled in the rotunda of the United States capitol in 1841, it prompted both considerable praise and scathing criticism. People were outraged that Greenough depicted the nation's first president half naked with a Roman-style toga covering his lower torso, making him look like a Parnasian god or a caricatured figure from the classical past instead of a contemporary hero. The concept for the piece was the idea of "an idiot," one reporter for the *New York Herald* asserted.[7] And it cost a fortune, more than twice as much as had been anticipated. Even Greenough didn't think the piece was effective in the rotunda, which he felt was much too dark. He therefore proposed putting it outside on the east lawn, a change he was able to effect after intensely lobbying Congress. But to many people it looked even worse there, as the sun now embarrassingly highlighted Washington's evident nudity while the elements discolored the marble and created multiple cracks. Nonetheless, the statue remained in this unsympathetic location until 1908, when it was further demeaned by being transferred to the Smithsonian Institution, a neo-Gothic building whose style Greenough despised. And to make matters worse, in 1964, it was moved to the newly constructed Museum of History and Technology (now the National Museum of American History) where it was placed next to an escalator that takes visitors to a basement cafeteria.

One of the most vehemently contested pieces of public art in recent times was, of course, Maya Lin's *Vietnam Veterans Memorial* on the mall in Washington. Veteran's groups hated Lin's winning proposal long before it was built in 1982 because, in their opinion, it was merely a black, somber, abstract mass sunken into the ground like an abandoned tombstone and thus a painful symbol of death and defeat, not the heroism and honor that they believed a war monument should convey. They did not stop their ferocious attacks until a realistic statue of three Vietnam vets by Frederick Hart was installed nearby. The outrage they expressed, while often vitriolic, was not without precedent, as government-sponsored monuments in the twentieth century had frequently been the subject of public distain. "Is This Statuary Worth More Than a Million of Your Money?" cried an article in *ARTNews* in 1955 following an exposé of federal government commissions.[8] Some of the reporter's most biting words were directed at Felix de Weldon's *Marine Corps Memorial* based on Joe Rosenthal's famous World War II photograph of soldiers raising the American flag over Iwo Jima on February 23, 1945. She called it "artistically appalling," being particularly insulted by its "stylistic resemblance to sculptural monuments of the Nazis and the Soviets."[9] But history is as fickle as it is instructive. For this once-reviled piece was soon considered one of the country's most moving, its place in history recently reaffirmed by the World Trade Center disaster and the much publicized photograph of New York firefighters raising the flag over Ground Zero like their Marine counterparts in the Pacific years earlier. Maya Lin's elegant, emotive monument experienced a similar reversal of fortune, and is now one of the most celebrated pieces of public art in the U.S., attracting more visitors than any other site in Washington and more imitations across the country than Lin undoubtedly would have wanted.

Another hotly contested piece was Richard Serra's *Tilted Arc* on Federal Plaza in lower Manhattan. Installed, ironically, just a year before Lin's memorial, after a lengthy competition presided over by a panel of experts, the 120-foot-long torqued span of Cor-Ten steel was unceremoniously destroyed in 1989 when federal workers in the building won a bitter court case against the artist and his work. Although he will forever be associated with this sculpture and the controversy it provoked, Serra has gone on to create even more impressive work and has been almost universally acclaimed since that disaster as one of the most important sculptors of our time, perhaps of the entire twentieth century, though this later success has been achieved primarily in the realm of galleries and museums.

For all of their historical and cultural importance, however, these changes in opinion, while instructive, generally mean very little when it comes to placing new art in new locales. That is because most people in the U.S. have never heard of Richard Serra, no less his *Tilted Arc*. And what they don't know doesn't hurt them, at least in their opinion. People do know what they like, and what they like is what they want, and what they want is what they demand, no matter what history or experts may say. Most people are also set against change, which has led to extreme applications of the NIMBY ("not in my back yard") phenomenon, such as the protests of Upper West Side residents of Manhattan against the Rose Center for Earth and Space designed by James Polshek for the American Museum of Natural History.[10]

That does not mean the public has no tolerance for art that is challenging. As Thomas Crow has observed, "the public," at least those who go to museums (in greater numbers than to all sports events in the U.S. combined), is not an elite but a decidedly mixed lot.[11] Moreover, as Crow also affirmed, people still attend exhibitions of difficult and demanding work, as evident from *Matthew Barney: The Cremaster Cycle* at the Guggenheim Museum in New York in 2003. Although that show may have been the ultimate in spectacle, it nonetheless was dense, complicated, and uncompromising. Yet it was surprisingly successful, attracting more visitors than any exhibition the Guggenheim had ever staged, except for its infamous *The Art of the Motorcycle* show in 1998.[12] It is therefore not a simple question of an unbridgeable divide between a philistine public who hates contemporary art and an enlightened culturati who supports it. Even the culturati do not form a unified group of like-minded elites, as its radically divided opinions about the Barney show–and *Tilted Arc*–make clear.

That being said, it is still true that most people gravitate toward art that makes them feel good, which generally means art that they can contextualize and understand. Any exhibition that deals with Impressionism is thus destined to be a blockbuster, and representational work has almost always been popular. But in our curiously divided moment, while Impressionism remains a consistent winner at the box office, representational art has often been considered as pugnacious and offensive as anything else that has been produced, even when it does not deal with sensitive issues such as sexuality, politics, and religion.

Nowhere is this more clearly demonstrated than in a series of outdoor exhibitions of sculpture held between 2000 and 2003 in Santa Barbara, California, a city of considerable wealth and sophistication that has long enjoyed an enviable reputation for its support of the arts. The exhibitions, funded solely from the city's annual budget, were part of an ambitious, three-year program to bring contemporary art to State Street, the city's main, *ramblas*-like artery that was being renovated. Specific sites on the newly bricked sidewalks were designated to receive relatively large-scale work, given different paving patterns, and equipped with special, subsurface support mechanisms. The first exhibition was a group show of established artists from across the country–Deborah Butterfield, Bryan Hunt, Jim Dine, Robert Hudson, and James Surls. It was very well received. Everyone was pleased.

The following year, Meg Linton, then director of the Contemporary Arts Forum in the city, organized a show of six works by the Mexican-American artist Luis Jimenez–boldly painted fiberglass sculptures of a dancing Mexican cowboy and cowgirl, a mixed-race steelworker, a bucking mustang, a group of howling alligators, a Native American man and woman in a pieta pose, and a Mexican man carrying a woman in what Jimenez described as a border crossing. Lively, accessible, and deeply human, these works set off a maelstrom that seemed to know no bounds. People called them "monstrosities," "hideous," "garish," "grotesque," "awful," "tasteless," and "vulgar."[13] The whirlwind of invective subsided only when the show ended and the sculptures were shipped back to their former locations around the country. The town reclaimed its violated center and breathed a collective sigh of relief.

The following year, the last the budget was intended to cover, William Tucker agreed to be the featured artist. Tucker, now a naturalized U.S. citizen, had been one of England's leading sculptors, representing Great Britain at the Venice Biennale in the 1970s and receiving major awards and commissions for the next three decades. Tucker's recent sculptures have become increasingly figurative, drawing for inspiration on such early modern masters as Rodin and Degas. His work is in museums and galleries around the world. The exhibition in Santa Barbara consisted of nine of his sculptures, most of which had just come from an important retrospective at the Henry Moore Sculpture Park in England, one of the most distinguished venues in that country. Tucker had no idea of what was soon to occur.

Before the exhibition even opened, the *Santa Barbara News-Press*, the city's primary newspaper, ran a front-page photograph, above the fold, in which a woman appeared to be retching in front of one of his sculptures. That was just the beginning. The town was infuriated with Tucker's work, which one resident claimed "offer[s] nothing but bewilderment and frustration."[14] Others were more condemning, as they found the work to be "insulting dino doo-doo" and "the ugliest sculpture that I have ever seen."[15] Even the art critic for the paper admitted that the sculptures "have been called names you never heard in the Bible."[16] One writer suggested that the works be dropped on Iraq as America's cultural present to that country while others applauded when vandals toppled one of the bronzes, claiming the hooligans were actually performing a public service.[17] The newspaper seemed to encourage this kind of thinking–controversy being good for circulation. Only the converted came to the various public lectures on Tucker and his work; everyone else began to long for the now seemingly benign Jimenez. Anything was better than Tucker's feces-evoking forms. Someone even took the official brochure the city had produced, scanned it, replaced the text with derogatory commentary on each work, and put copies of the new look-alike brochure where the official ones were supposed to go. As with the Jimenez show, the community's anger continued to the closing, which was supposed to have been after Halloween but was moved up to avoid any other vandalism (though officials claimed it was to get the sculptures back to Tucker's studio before rains made dirt roads in his neighborhood impassable). Needless to say, the public's outrage forced the city council to reconsider its support of any future art initiative on State Street unless it focused on local artists, although it was unclear whether that would prevent objections from their constituents.

These tales of woe are painfully familiar, as they have been spun in cities and towns across the country. Residents of Newburyport, Massachusetts, for example, were recently enraged by a piece of sculpture consisting of ten modest-size, rocklike pieces of Styrofoam (that to some looked like garbage bags) floating in a pond on the town green, an effort, according to the artist, to draw attention to political and environmental issues that the town had refused to address. Bending to public pressure, the town's board of selectmen voted to terminate the exhibition halfway through its agreed-upon duration.[18] Important members of the arts community in Boston would have been thrilled if a similar fate had befallen the *Irish Famine Memorial* that was erected in 1998 at considerable private expense on downtown Washington Street. "It's an embarrassment," claimed Pallas Lombardi, then executive director of the Cambridge Arts Council. "A clichéd melodrama," according to Nick Capasso, curator at the DeCordova Museum and Sculpture Park in Lincoln, Massachusetts.[19] Christine Temin, chief art critic for the *Boston Globe* went ever further, calling it a "crude caricature...that insults those it is supposed to honor...its thudding literalness...surpassed only by its condescension."[20] On a national level, consider the controversy surrounding the memorial for World War II veterans proposed for the mall in Washington. Or the debate about Ground Zero in New York.

It is difficult to generalize about all of these projects, but it is clear that each generated heated exchanges and plenty of ill will. It is also evident that the number of stakeholders has dramatically increased, as has the intensity of their opinions. Although due at least in part to the sheer growth in the population, this expanded constituency and its heightened interest in public art is also the product of a host of other factors–keener interest in land use and the shrinking number of available sites for sculpture, greater sophistication about process and the arts, concerns about the use of public funds or the rights of individual donors, the desire to create underpinnings for community, even political correctness. Has this become the norm? Are the dichotomous tensions of our moment fostering a public that creates this kind of squabbling every time works of art are placed in public spaces? The answer, happily, is no; there are plenty of contrary examples.

Over the past fifteen years, for instance, the city of Hamilton, Ohio, which lies halfway between Cincinnati and Dayton, has acquired and installed more than thirty pieces of sculpture in a 265-acre park that is the pride of the community. In 2000, the governor of Ohio, following the wishes of residents, officially named Hamilton the "City of Sculpture." Surprisingly, perhaps, all but a few of the works in the park are nonrepresentational, thus debunking the widely held notion that the unfamiliar is automatically objectionable, a point underscored as well by the number of sculpture parks that have recently arisen across the country in which abstract art plays major roles.

Equally successful, though much less surprising, has been the seemingly endless proliferation of sculptures by J. Seward Johnson Jr., life-size cast metal sculptures of individuals and groups based on iconic works of art, such as Edouard Manet's *Dejeuner sur l'herbe* and Claude Monet's *Terrace at Saint-Adresse*. Santa Barbara has no fewer than three examples. The Corcoran Museum even gave Johnson a solo exhibition in 2003. Or consider the parade of cow sculptures that have invaded cities in the United States since 1999 when Chicago decided to imitate Berne, Switzerland, and invited artists to decorate precast bovines that were then set on the sidewalks of the city's main shopping districts. Other than an eloquent critique by Roberta Smith of the *New York Times*, these herds have been the victim of few dissenting voices.[21] In fact, they have been so popular that they have multiplied across the country, showing up in Baltimore, Dallas, Orlando, Tampa, Los Angeles, Saint Louis, and Cedar Rapids in the summer of 2001 alone, while some municipalities (such as Boston, Providence, Rhode Island, and Saratoga Springs, New York) tried to separate themselves from the pack and substituted fish, sheep, horses, pigs, and birds, all of which were enthusiastically embraced by their respective communities. Fun, fresh (at least in the beginning), and nonthreatening, the cows and their compatriots are the homespun counterparts to the *tilted arcs* of the world, something that seems to have grown up naturally from local concerns and popular interest. In many cases, they have even been auctioned off after being exhibited to raise money for arts organizations and social causes.

There is a serious problem with the charge of these bovines, however. For no matter how appealing or economically rewarding they may be, they cannot and should not be taken as the standard for public art. As Roberta Smith stated, "It is 'a supposedly fun thing' that, one hopes, the city will never do again," because the more they procreate, the more they become the norm, making it difficult for more legitimate work to take their place.

In contrast, *Vita Brevis* is to be warmly welcomed; it has proven to be the perfect vehicle for advancing avant-garde art and arts education without sacrificing quality or provoking negative backlash. Its success is due to a number of factors. It has engaged diverse communities in Boston and drawn strength from local organizations–the National Park Service and Boston's Parks and Recreation Department, along with many of the city's important historic sites. It has focused on local phenomena, such as Frederick Law Olmsted's Emerald Necklace and the Freedom Trail. And, like the cows, it has the distinct advantage of being temporary, so no matter what someone might think of a particular work, relief, eventually, is guaranteed. Equally important, participating artists have been drawn from broad-based constituencies–local, national, and international pools–thus leveling the geographic field. The selected artists have been of all ages with as many women as men. The artists have dealt with cutting-edge issues, often with advanced technology, but have not aggressively imposed on their sites, with the possible exception of Krzysztof Wodiczko's projection on the Bunker Hill Monument about the so-called code of silence in the Boston neighborhood of Charlestown. Moreover, the works have been highly intelligent and aesthetically charged, remarkably crafted and professionally maintained. And best of all perhaps, given the embarrassing shortage of contemporary art in Boston, particularly the lack of twentieth-century outdoor sculpture, Vita Brevis has helped to fill a glaring gap in the city. Boston may never reclaim a leadership role in its support of the art of our era. It thereby may never recover the stature it enjoyed in the nineteenth century or that it still relishes in other fields–science, medicine, higher education, even the culinary arts. But it is a terrific place to start, especially in this curious, contradictory moment, when daring and creativity could not be more precious or desired.

1 Over the past ten years, the United States government has issued 60,884,784 passports. (See http:travel.state.gov/passport_statistics.html.) However, it is impossible to determine how many of these were replacements for ones lost or stolen or how many were renewals for those that were issued with a five-year lifespan. On the growth of the fitness industry, according to Fei Mei Chan, "A Ton of Prevention. The Fitness Industry," forbes.com, May, 8, 2002, the sale of exercise machinery to homeowners climbed from $1.9 billion in 1990 to $5.8 billion in 2000. The Sporting Goods Manufacturers Association also reported that growth in health club memberships in the U.S. rose from 13.8 million in 1987 to 22.5 million in 1998, a 63% gain. See "Fitness Equipment Drives Sporting Goods Growth," at www.sgma.com/press/1999/press985880699-19304.html. As for obesity, see Nancy Wartik, "Rising Obesity in Children Prompts Call to Action," *New York Times*, August 26, 2003, F5. For SAT scores see, collegeboard.com and *New York Daily News*, August 27, 2003, p. 19. On the Mono Lake discovery see, Richard Hoover et al., "Spirochaeta Americana sp. nov., a new haloalkaliphilic, obligately anaerobic spirochaete isolated from soda Mono Lake in California," *International Journal of Systematic and Evolutionary Microbiology*, 2003, vol. 53, p. 815-21, and http://science.nasa.gov/headlines/y2003/30 jul_monolake.htm.

2 Among the candidates for the California Governorship were Angelyne, a 70-something, self-made, Los Angeles billboard queen, the former child television star Garry Coleman, Mary Carey, a 21 year old porn star who wanted to make lap dancing tax deductible, and Hollywood's man of steel, Arnold Schwarzenegger, whose entrance (unprecedentedly announced on *The Tonight Show*) caused Donald Isseui to withdraw from the race in tears. Isseui, a rich, disgruntled Republican congressman, financed the initial recall initiative with the hope he would be able to run virtually uncontested against Gray Davis, the elected Democratic governor who had come under such political fire that even his own party was questioning his behavior. Edward Said's assertion is in his essay "Global Crisis is Over Iraq," which appeared in Lawrence Rinder, ed., *The American Effect. Global Perspectives on the United States, 1990-2003*, exhibition catalogue, Whitney Museum of Art, 2003, p.179. Among other observers who affirm an increasing polarization in America, see Nicholas D. Kristof, "Believe It, or Not," *New York Times*, August 15, 2003, A29. From surveys Kristof consulted, he noted the widening gap between the U.S. and other industrial nations when it comes to faith. "Religion," he asserted, "remains central to American life, and is getting more so, in a way that is true of no other [industrialized] country in the world with the possible exception of South Korea." But what he found even more disturbing is the divide that has simultaneously increased between "intellectual and religious America," calling it "poisonous," largely because it meant yet another "growing polarization within our society."

3 Kevin Phillips, *Wealth and Democracy. A Political History of the American Rich*, New York, Broadway Books, 2002, p. 103. Also see pp. 127-38, 427-28, and 361, where he notes that "the top 1 percent pocketed 42 percent of the stock market gains between 1989 and 1997, while the top 10 percent of the population took 86 percent."

4 Department of Transportation via informationplease.com/ipa/A0004727.html. According to the agency, 235,331,000 motor vehicles were registered in 2001 (the last year statistics were available; the number also includes trucks and buses). In 1990, there were 193,057,000, an increase of more than 40,000,000 or about 20 percent. Increased mobility comes at considerable cost. A recent study of traffic jams in the U.S. estimated that time spent in gridlock conditions had a $68 million price tag. See *USA Today*, October 3, 2003.

5 See "Betrayal by Cell Phone," CBSNEWS.com, September 29, 2003. Also see James E. Katz and Mark Aakhaus, eds., *Perpetual Contact: Mobile Communication, Private Talk, Public Performance*, Cambridge, Cambridge University Press, 2002, pp. 5 and 80, where it is noted that the wireless data market was estimated to rise from a $1.8 billion industry in 1999 to a staggering $13.2 billion in 2003. Presently, over 40 percent of Americans rely on cell phones with the numbers in Europe and Asia considerably higher. "Table 1.1 Estimates of mobile phone ownership," in Katz & Aakhaus, p.5; the table is taken from *Financial Times*, June 14, 2001, p.26.

6 On Greenough and this fated sculpture see, Nathalia Wright, *Horatio Greenough: The First American Sculptor*, Philadelphia, University of Pennsylvania, 1963, 117–59; Wayne Craven, *Sculpture in America*, New York, Thomas Crowell Co., 1964, 103–09; and Sylvia E. Crane, *White Silence; Greenough, Powers, and Crawford, American Sculptors in Nineteenth-Century Italy*, Coral Gables, University of Miami Press, 1972, pp. 69–85. For a fascinating discussion of its political implications see Fred Saddler, "Body Impolitic; Cultural Hierarchy in a Democratic Age," *Gazette Newsletter of the Mid-Atlantic Popular/American Cultural Association*, December 2001.

7 The article, cited in Wright, p. 144, appeared on December 6, 1841.

8 Charlotte Devree, "Is This Statuary Worth More Than a Million of Your Money?" *ARTnews*, vol. 54, April 1955, p. 34. Also see Sanka Knox, "Public Sculpture in US Deplored," *New York Times*, March 31, 1955.

9 For negative commentary at the initial hearing about the monument, see Karal Ann Marling and John Wetenhall, *Iwo Jima: Monuments, Memories, and the American Hero*, Cambridge, MA, Harvard University Press, 1991.

10 Museum officials conducted over 250 meetings with Upper West Side residents in order to quell concerns about the Rose Center's design and impact. See Glenn Collins, "Outer Space vs. Parking Space. Planetarium and Wary Neighbors Prepare for Opening," *New York Times*, January 25, 2000, B1. When it opened, the Rose Center was universally hailed as one of the great buildings of our time.

11 Thomas Crow, *The Rise of the Sixties. American and European Art in the Era of Dissent*, New York, Harry N. Abrams, p. 7.

12 *The Cremaster Cycle* attracted an average of 18,206 visitors weekly and 300,206 visitors total. *The Art of the Motorcycle* show had an average of 23,897 visitors weekly and 301,037 visitors total. Attendance figures courtesy of the Guggenheim Museum, New York.

13 Letters to the editor, *Santa Barbara New-Press*, July 31, 2001, D1, p. 4, 6.

14 John Sandberg, "Metal Sculptures Leave Him Cold," *Santa Barbara New-Press*, May 11, 2002, A10.

15 Barney Brantingham, "Don't like the new art? Tell the mayor," *Santa Barbara New-Press*, May 10, 2002, B1.

16 Josef Woodard, "Going Public," *Santa Barbara New-Press*, June 1, 2002, D1.

17 Melre Betz, "A critical look at art vandalism," *Santa Barbara New-Press*, June 13, 2002, A12.

18 John McElhenny, "Art floats, but not for long," *Boston Globe*, July 28, 2003, B1.

19 Christine Temin, "The Public's Art? The Irish Famine Memorial Is the Result of a Weak, Private Process That Needs To Be Changed," *Boston Globe*, August 30, 1998, N1.

20 Ibid.

21 Roberta Smith, "Stretching Definitions of Outdoor Sculpture," *New York Times*, July 28, 2000, E27. Also see Stephen Kinzer, "Art on Streets Till the Cows Come Home," *New York Times*, August 20, 2001.

Park Setting Time
by John Stilgoe
Orchard Professor in the History of Landscape
at Harvard University

Cows still shape aesthetics. On Boston Common, municipal park trees are still pruned to what farmers call the *browse line*, the height above which cows cannot reach to munch leaves and destroy branches. Pedestrians, long ignorant of browsing cows, stroll beneath the arched branches and enjoy an idealized rural landscape of stylized pasture and meadow. No one thinks much today about the early nineteenth-century agrarian landscape, rural values, or even cows.

Parks work a special magic. By being old fashioned, just a little out of date, they enable a very special kind of creativity. Parks sharpen the imagination by restoring a fertile distance from immediacy, from the strains of daily life in complex times.

Late in the nineteenth century a furious debate developed about the use of urban parks. In many cities, parks had become the "center for all sorts of noisy sports, for festivities of the brass band, fireworks, and barbaric order," complained an anonymous writer in an 1889 *Garden and Forest* article. Almost everyone, asserted the writer, seemed to have forgotten the "true" purpose of the parks created only three decades earlier. An urban park ought to be "a place where the urban inhabitants can, to the fullest extent, obtain the genuine recreation coming from the peaceful enjoyment of an idealized rural landscape, in rest-giving contrast to their wonted existence amidst the city's turmoil." But clearly a lot of inhabitants liked the baseball games and the band concerts, and the writer admitted understanding the growing perplexity of mayors, city councilors, and park-department superintendents. No matter what the use, authorities received complaints.

Nowadays historians focus chiefly on the origins of the park movement, and in particular pay special homage to the creation of Central Park in New York. But the subsequent history of urban parks deserves scrutiny, too, for the ways city dwellers use parks is not always the way pioneer park-makers envisioned. In Boston, an extraordinary urban amenity, strategically placed midway between the former Navy Yard and the former Watertown Arsenal, has its origin in military thinking almost as long-forgotten as browsing cows. The Charles River Basin began as a United States Navy initiative to store warships in fresh water just adjacent to the Charlestown Navy Yard. Freshwater mooring made a cost-effective barnacle-prevention technique. The basin that now shimmers in morning and afternoon light, the immense reach of open water that brings easterly gales deep into the land and provides a splendid environment for fireworks and open-air music and small-boat pleasure, originated as part of a weapons system. MBTA Red Line riders no more notice the warship-size drawbridge in the middle of the

Charles River viaduct than tourists enjoying rides in refurbished World War II amphibious assault vehicles think about the propriety of such military weapons cruising the fresh-water expanse above the dam. No one ponders the irony of the Charles River Dam lock being too narrow for most pre-Great War warships. Whatever contemporary Americans think of their super-power military, they almost never consider parks and park-making in military terms. Historians rarely comment either, even though the British redcoats camped and maneuvered on Boston Common and built an artillery range in its northwest corner.

The preservation of Boston Common, too rarely discussed in the history of United States urban park-making, is critical to finding a longer view of park usage.

The Common originated as a place to collect cows. Boston families fortunate enough to own cows milked them in the morning and then led them to the Common. During the day herders took the cows to pasture, and in late afternoon brought them back to the Common, where children collected them and brought them home for evening milking. The cows did not actually graze on the Common. Forty acres did not provide enough grass to feed very many cows, but forty acres proved a very roomy collection and dispersal point. By virtue of its location, the Common hosted other activities: political and religious speeches and sermons, open-air elections, even hangings. Eventually the British Army, which quartered its troops in nearby private homes and so earned the enmity of Bostonians, exercised on it before and during the siege of Boston by the Continental Army. After Independence the cows remained, but in decreasing number, and the growth of the city made driving the animals to and from pasture an increasingly time-consuming occupation.

The memory of cow-keeping inspired the preservation of the Common, although the term *cow pasture*, like tales of Boston streets originating as cow paths, became the material of folklore. "Boston owes its only park worth the name–the celebrated Common–to the necessity of leaving a convenient cow-pasture for the babes and sucklings of that now mature community," reported an anonymous *Atlantic Monthly* writer in 1861. "May the memory of the weaning babes who pleaded for the spot where their 'milky mothers' fed be ever sacred in our Athens, and may the cows of Boston be embalmed with the bulls of Egypt! A white heifer should be perpetually grazing, at her tether, in the shadow of the Great Elm." But *how* did anyone actually care about the cows? What was so important about the cows that adult Bostonians so forcefully advocated preserving a tree-studded but otherwise scarcely adorned forty acres?

Bostonians, perhaps especially Boston men, insisted on "preserving" the Common because they recalled with deep pleasure their boyhood freedom to play in it, to shape it, to do just about as they pleased with a tract of land adults ordinarily avoided. But once preserved, the preservers found themselves in a quandary. How should the City address the absence of the cows? The *Atlantic Monthly* writer only half-seriously suggested tethering a heifer in the Common as a reminder of the past. "Would it be wholly unbecoming one born in full view of that lovely enclosure to suggest that the straightness of the lines in which the trees are planted on Boston Common, and the rapidly increasing thickness of their foliage, destroy in the summer season the effect of breadth and liberty, hide both the immediate and distant landscape, stifle the breeze, and diminish the attractiveness of the spot?" Something had gone wrong. "Fewer trees, scattered in clumps and paying little regard to paths, would vastly improve the effect." In 1861, as the Civil War deepened into bloodbath and irrevocable error, the *Atlantic Monthly* writer worried about tree-planting on the Common.

Urban park-making, at least according to expert historians, gathered force as the Union threatened to fragment. But historians almost never focus on the national context of the first park-making effort: the deepening fear of constitutional crisis and ensuing Civil War. While the late-nineteenth-century national-park movement is now in a political and cultural context that spans subjects from panorama photography to Teddy Roosevelt to rugged individualism to railroad-industry tourist advertising, the wider context of early urban park-making exists in a sort of limbo. What prompted the anonymous critic to complain about straight-line tree-planting on Boston Common? Why the focus on retrospection, on valuing something that was disappearing? Why seriously suggest that a heifer might be tethered under the trees?

Consider in the context of the present era the curious dichotomy in the career of Central Park creator Frederick Law Olmsted. In his 1857 *Journey Through Texas: Or, A Saddle-Trip on the Southwestern Frontier*, one of several books he published based on carefully recorded travels in the slave-holding states, Olmsted wrote, "This large district, extending from the Trinity River to the bayous of the Mississippi, has, throughout, the same general characteristics, the principal of which are, lowness, flatness, and wetness. The soil is variable, but is in greater part a loose, sandy loam, covered with coarse grasses, forming level prairies, which are everywhere broken by belts of pine forests, usually bordering creeks and bayous, but often standing in islands."

The bayous troubled Olmsted. The poor roads, often the corduroy type made of logs laid side by side atop mud, led him further into adventure than he originally intended. "The river-bottoms, still lower than the general level, are subject to constant overflow by tide-water, and what with the fallen timber, the dense undergrowth, the mire-quags, the abrupt gullies, and patches of rotten or floating corduroy, and three or four feet of dirty salt-water, the roads through them are not such as one would choose for a morning ride." Instead of pursuing his intended mission of examining the economy of the region, he found himself confronting an ecosystem very unlike that of New York City. "The many pools, through which the usual track took us, were swarming with venomous water-snakes, four or five black moccasins often lifting at once their devilish heads above the dirty surface, and wriggling about our horses' heels. Beyond the Sabine, alligator holes are an additional excitement, the unsuspicious traveler suddenly sinking through the treacherous surface, and sometimes falling a victim, horse and all, to the hideous jaws of the reptile, while overwhelmed by the engulfing mire in which he lurks." Here Olmsted details travel in a genuine wilderness. "The avernal entrance might, I should think, with good probabilities, be looked for in this region," he concludes.

Certainly the region between the Trinity and Sabine rivers exists in Olmsted's writing as a natural wilderness only slightly modified by settlers unable to maintain the tortuous roads or *traces* they have built. However much twenty-first-century readers might see it as a very rich ecosystem, Olmsted saw the region as excruciatingly difficult to describe in words. While its general characteristics express themselves in words that early-nineteenth-century educated readers expected to see in topographical description–words like *flatness*, *loam*, *prairie* and perhaps *creeks* and *bayous*–spots peculiar to it required creative writing. *Quags*, for example, is scarcely an ordinary term, and *alligator hole* existed chiefly as a localism. In 1859, when John Russell Bartlett published his *Dictionary of Americanism: A Glossary of Words and Phrases Usually Regarded as Peculiar to the United States*, even *alligator* demanded lexicographical attention. "A large American reptile, resembling the Egyptian crocodile, having a wide, obtuse muzzle and unequal teeth," begins his definition. "Though still numerous in Florida, Louisiana, and Texas, they are no longer regarded as very dangerous." But alligators frightened Olmsted thoroughly, and those he saw seemed perfectly able to kill both horse and rider already terrified and floundering in engulfing mire.

Such is a perfect metaphor for the position in which so many educated people in the United States found themselves in the late 1850s. No longer did the Constitution seem able to contain the deepening sectional animosity triggered first by tariff controversy and manufacturing, then by westward expansion, then by antislavery agitation. No matter what the issue–nullification, abolitionism, expansionism, even building the transcontinental railroad–utterly intractable Constitutional problems stymied Webster, Calhoun, Clay, and other great politicians while making ordinary citizens increasingly pessimistic. In the 1850s, Americans found themselves heading for disaster. Unable to avoid one crisis after another, their best statesmen fumbled for words to describe the national predicament.

In this period flourished not only the Hudson River School of painting and a second-rate art derivative of it–say, Currier and Ives lithographs–but a fast-growing desire to look backward at a seemingly less complicated, almost peaceful existence. Great landscape painting of the ante-bellum era depicts an idealized rural landscape or a wilderness being converted into the shaped land that is designated as *landscape*. By the late 1850s, more and more educated Americans longed for something past in ways nostalgia fails to accurately connote. They did not so much want rural life: after all, many had deliberately moved to cities. They did not so much want an economy minus factories, steam engines, and railroads: many profited from such technologies. And they did not so much want a Spartan simplicity: many desired fine paintings on their walls, and many others prized plaster walls over unfinished logs. But a vast number wanted some sense of peace, some escape from continuous political stress, some inkling of a positive 1860s. About the only way they found that sense of peace was to look backward, to look deep and long at paintings exemplifying an earlier, simpler republic well grounded in rural affairs.

Then too, at least in Boston, they could preserve the Common, thinking that somehow the cows might have vanished but the cow-browsed landscape could endure. The Common would be a portal into something else, something more-or-less known but offering more-or-less pleasant surprises, some wildflowers, maybe a hawk, harlequin-colored leaves in autumn.

"Cold houses, coarse food unskillfully cooked, long winters, harsh springs, however favorable to the heroism of the stomach, the lungs, and the spirits, are not found conducive to longevity. In like manner, monotony, seclusion, lack of variety and of social stimulus lower the tone of humanity, drive to sensual pleasures and secret vices, and nourish a miserable pack of mean and degrading immoralities, of which scandal, gossip, backbiting, tale-bearing are the better examples." So concludes the anonymous *Atlantic Monthly* critic of the rural life so many Bostonians had deliberately left behind for *urbanity*. "Political freedom, popular education, the circulation of newspapers, books, engravings, pictures, have already created a public which understands that man does not live by bread alone, which demands leisure, beauty, space, architecture, landscape, music, elegance, with an imperative voice, and is ready to back its demands with the necessary self-taxation." In cities such wondrous goods might be had, and would be had, if Central Park proved any indicator.

In calling Central Park "a royal work, undertaken and achieved by the Democracy," the *Atlantic Monthly* writer introduced both the concept of enlightened despotism and the designer and first superintendent of the Park, Frederick Law Olmsted. Together with his partner, Calvert Vaux, Olmsted won the 1858 design competition for the park, and by 1861 had the satisfaction of seeing construction far enough along for the people of New York to enjoy. "If he had not been born, as an agriculturist, and as the keenest, most candid, and instructive of all our writers on the moral and political economy of our American Slavery, a name to be long remembered, he might safely trust his reputation to the keeping of New York City and all her successive citizens, as the author and achiever of the Central Park," proclaimed the *Atlantic Monthly* writer of a man whose "union of prosaic sense with poetical feeling, of democratic sympathies with refined and scholarly tastes, of punctilious respect for facts with tender hospitality for ideas" enabled him to carry forward an awesome enterprise in the midst of an awesome Civil War. Four years after publishing his account of riding among alligators and water moccasins, Olmsted managed to create and maintain an oasis of calm in the midst of New York just as the republic thrashed into political quagmire.

Central Park is an idealized rural landscape, not a formal palace garden, not what Boston Common might have become had the paths been further straightened and more trees planted alongside them. Names like *The Ramble* and *Sheep Meadow* announce the idealization, and the idealization succeeded beyond the wildest imagining. Civil War veterans returned not only to enjoy the park but to want a piece of it themselves, to move to the borderlands, to what eventually were called suburbs. On half-acre or one-acre lots, families recreated the idealized farm of yore. The front lawn became the meadow regularly mowed, the back lawn the pasture for substitute livestock, the dog and the cat. A vegetable garden represented arable fields, and a fruit tree or two memorialized the orchard. Civil War veterans swept out along the railroad lines and commuted to work. Newly arrived immigrants swept into their vacated places, living in tenements and enjoying parks without realizing that the parks subtly reoriented their children toward moving to streetcar suburbs, railroad suburbs, exurbia. A huge, two-generational population flow occurred in the aftermath of the Civil War, when urban amenities lost the race with urban distress–with 'stress. By the late 1880s, no one knew how to manage urban parks, yet everyone championed building more.

The 1889 *Garden and Forest* writer knew the crisis but missed its point. While urban park-making began in ante-bellum political distress and incorporated an idealized landscape into an oasis of urban balm, by the 1880s too few urban Americans remembered or cared about the rural landscape of 1835. Many park users no longer did demanding physical labor six days a week and no longer wanted to relax in parks. Instead, they sat at desks and typewriters and wanted active recreation on their days and evenings off, which walking, at first, satisfied. No wonder mayors, city councilors, and park-department superintendents puzzled over the making of new parks and the maintenance of existing ones. While many Boston citizens agreed with Olmsted that the city's parks existed essentially to "provide opportunity for a form of recreation to be obtained only through the influence of pleasing natural scenery upon the sensibilities of those quietly contemplating it," others insisted on anything but contemplation.

In the middle of the debate, everyone confronted massive ecological change. The chestnut blight, then Dutch elm disease, wiped out entire species of trees, and immigrant bird species, the English sparrow and the starling, displaced native songbirds. Small-scale change altered affairs too. Damming the Charles River around 1910 changed the Fens forever. The tidal marsh Olmsted worried about incorporating into the larger park system nicknamed "the emerald necklace" became a curvilinear park focused on fresh-water pools surrounded by marsh, something straight out of Lincolnshire, perhaps, but just possibly out of the region between the Sabine and Trinity rivers. Almost suddenly, thoughtful park-goers realized that parks could change and would have to change, and change swirled around them. By the turn of the century, people saw the value of species diversity and the enduring wisdom of creating parks with multiple, overlying ecosystems.

From about 1890 to 1920, the people of Massachusetts, especially Bostonians, developed a sophisticated approach to park design and, far more importantly, to park change. On the one hand, they created dozens of playgrounds and athletic fields, many of them with specialized zones for active recreation classified by age. With more and more certainty and verve, they built parks for toddlers, for adolescents, and for teenagers and adults involved in league sports. In 1901, for example, they built forty-two tennis courts at Franklin Field, an active-recreation adjunct to Franklin Park, a massive park built between 1885 and 1895. At the same time, through the Metropolitan Park Commission, they opened outlying reservations as miniature wilderness parks, perhaps the best examples being the Blue Hills and the Middlesex Fells. On the other hand, they incorporated new activities into parks previously used essentially for strolling and looking, putting a boathouse on Jamaica Pond in 1895 and a golf course in Franklin Park in 1902, for instance, and creating the Franklin Park Zoo in 1915 and the Franklin Park Rose Garden in 1925. The Great Depression ended the series of experiments in 1930 and challenged taxpayers to care for what they had built, but long afterward most people accepted the general concept of adapting parks to changing public needs.

So complex is the post-1890 period that many historians rarely write about it, let alone ponder its accomplishments. Consider snakes and alligators. In the Blue Hills Reservation, rattlesnakes are a protected species, and not particularly reticent about alarming hikers and horseback riders. Alligators live in Franklin Park, although not on the golf course. What Olmsted found in coastal Texas in the late 1850s, any Bostonian can find today, thanks to public park systems that simultaneously protect an endangered species of dangerous, indigenous snake in one park while displaying alien alligators in the zoo in another. Neither dangerous snakes nor alligators figure much in the ante-bellum idealized-rural-landscape tradition, but both belong in the post-1890 understanding of parks as inclusive of ecosystem diversity.

Park-making and park-maintaining efforts after about 1890 originate in the understanding of parks as places able to accommodate and even improve change. But how do parks incorporate change? By the 1970s many parks had advocacy groups denouncing change, perhaps especially change wrought by the automobile, crime, and failing maintenance. Yet in the early 1970s articles in *Landscape Architecture* and other magazines heralded the rediscovery of environmental art that arrests the strolling viewer, and by the end of the decade Christo's twenty-four-mile-long *Running Fence* had set many park advocates to rethinking what parks might become in the future. In the midst of spiraling inflation and energy crises the next moment of public-park dynamism was born.

Superb art acutely set in a public park arrests the passerby. It surprises, perhaps stuns, perhaps inveigles, perhaps seduces. It may puzzle, perplex, or please. But always it fixes one's attention, not as the alligators fixed Olmsted's attention in the 1850s or a Blue Hills rattlesnake fixes attention today, but in an equally commanding way.

The long tradition that lies behind the artwork that forms the armature of this volume is not the tradition of monuments. For decades after Independence, citizens of the new republic honored heroes like Washington and concepts like liberty by erecting monuments. At first located chiefly in Mount Auburn and other great garden cemeteries that preceded the urban park-making movement by a decade or two, the statuary memorialized the recent past. As the nineteenth century advanced, statuary found its way into parks and along parkways, and just as public opinion about park use broadened, so did the subject of monuments. Fundamentally national subjects like liberty gave way to memorializing Civil War efforts such as the African American soldiers led by Robert Gould Shaw and the possible discovery of North America, or at least Vinland, by Leif Erickson. The Shaw monument at the north end of the Common and the Ann Whitney statue of Erickson on the Commonwealth Avenue mall near the Muddy River are as much taken for granted now as the equestrian statue of Washington in the Public Garden. But siting such monuments involved much discussion, often very heated discussion, about the propriety of subject and placement alike. Should Washington face east or west? Did the Shaw monument deflect attention from the State House? Did Whitney's statue flaunt too much exposed muscle and virility? Dissent about the proper use of parks surfaced in one monument argument after another, then vanished in the first years of the 1920s as nearly everyone agreed that such monuments indeed belonged in parks—and as the monuments became increasingly subtle. Nowadays few walkers notice the monument in Boston Common given by the British in recognition of the World War II kindness shown by the city to sailors of the Royal Navy.

Being made to notice, stopping to notice, involves another tradition, that of the bosky dell studded with figures of monsters, the dark pool enlivened by a sculpture of a giant eel, the shrubbery subtly and perfectly planted into a maze that baffles those its attracts. *Art on the Emerald Necklace* belongs to this tradition, and its success explains a bit about the last three decades of fitful stops and starts in park-making and park-changing.

From the mid-1950s until the close of the 1980s, urban citizens everywhere in the United States experienced parks built or altered with novel materials. This time saw not only declining use of urban parks and massive problems resulting from long-deferred maintenance and repair, but a quirky attempt to integrate avant-garde, even futuristic, design theory with the far older tradition usually called *design with nature*. Park departments struggling with the repair of hundred-year-old brick walkways found themselves rebuilding ten-year-old railings and replacing new metal benches that were uncomfortably cold in winter and hot in summer with stone and wood seating. Low-to-the-ground lighting failed when buried in snow, and windswept ultra-lightweight lighting poles vibrated themselves into fracture. Puddles formed when novel drainage systems froze, and flimsy plastic gazebo roofs turned a sickly yellow. So rapidly did new materials come and go within a framework of changing aesthetic theory that historians are still grappling with explaining the post-1955 changes in Copley Square alone. Within half a human generation, one new park replaced another new park. But from the fits and starts emerged a mature understanding that parks nurture change rather than simply host it. As park designers shifted away from glitzy, short-lived novel materials to traditional, time-tested ones, they created and restored parks that energize the works of art placed within them.

Superb art not only attains power in a superb setting, it makes the setting even more powerful. The typical urban park is a work of art in its own right, even though generations of Americans have been inclined to think of it as largely natural. Landscape architects understand that while their art focuses on the arrangement of living things–chiefly plants, but by extension, the animals that find the arranged plants home or a good place to visit–the results of their art are scarcely natural. Citizens seek out parks for many reasons, to run or bicycle or walk or muse or see fireworks or play tennis or keep an eye on toddlers playing. But for whatever reason, they are entering a space that is different from the space around it, and in its difference the parkgoer is soothed, recreated, relaxed, energized. How this process works no one knows, and only in the last several years have medical scientists even taken formal note of it. But art improves the process.

Superb art encountered in the park by a mind in the process of enjoying the park arrests the psyche and reorients it. It reminds the psyche of the poverty of virtual reality by reintroducing the psyche to a sort of hyper-reality that finds expression in changed time and in delight.

In the park, which is ordered about the natural rhythms of the seasons, the day's weather, even the length or brevity of daylight, art not only accentuates the natural but reinforces the power of the human to be creative. In the park, art changes time the way it never does in museums that ordinarily contain, display, and preserve it. Even as the art makes the park surround it, so the art changes the frame of time in which it exists. Suddenly juxtaposing a new color or movement against the ever-changing "natural" colors and shapes the typical park visitor expects, the art commands an immediate attention and rewards a sustained one. Each individual flow of ideas shifts subtly, and in that shifting time, flow shifts, too.

And in most cases, it is accessible only to those who have entered the park in the first place. It is an incredible, stunning bonus.

Let Freedom Ring

The Inaugural ICA/Vita Brevis Project
September 1998

Conversation between Jim Hodges and Carole Anne Meehan about *Here We Are*, Let Freedom Ring, Inaugural ICA/Vita Brevis Project

Carole Anne Meehan – Was one of your early thoughts for this project to use a church?

Jim Hodges – Jill and I thought that somehow the project could involve a church community. Also, we thought a church structure would be a nicely defined space that I could do something with.

C.A.M. – And then you encountered the Old North Church while walking the Freedom Trail?

J.H. – Yes. While inside Old North my eye was drawn to the window behind the sanctuary and to the tree in the courtyard behind. And even now, that perspective is an important source of inspiration for me. Views up into trees play a big part in a series of photographic pieces I am working on now.

C.A.M. – It is interesting how being inside the church led you back outside, to the intimate courtyard behind. You have talked of your treatment of it as an "interior" space that is outside.

J.H. – I was very interested in the idea of passageway or of transitional space between locations. The church is a mark on the map, a destination, if you will. But leading up to this destination is the blank space between destinations. I guess I thought of the courtyard as a kind of corridor that could be affected by sound. This sound would place the emphasis on the individuals who are moving through that corridor at any given moment. The intent of my work here would be realized in their awareness of the sound. I wanted to emphasize the space as a passageway, but also as a resting point.

C.A.M. – Fortunately it was a beautiful, discrete space that could serve as both container and passageway in the way you describe.

J.H. – It offered that because of the two rows of trees and benches that were already there. It was a perfect place to affect something there with its built-in symmetry. The idea of having the work be somewhat transparent or invisible was important to me as well. And that passersby would hear the sounds made by the wind chimes, or not, would be completely a chance occurrence.

C.A.M. – Overall, was creating *Here We Are* a new way of working for you?

J.H. – I did feel that this was an opportunity for me to kind of push myself, and to allow myself to take some chances. When one is invited to do projects sometimes there is a welcome sense of openness. This is great for sustaining a liberated sense of approaching one's practice and one's work.

C.A.M. – How was this particular situation liberating?

J.H. – Well, I hadn't worked in a space like this before, nor with these materials. And it seemed that it would be OK for the

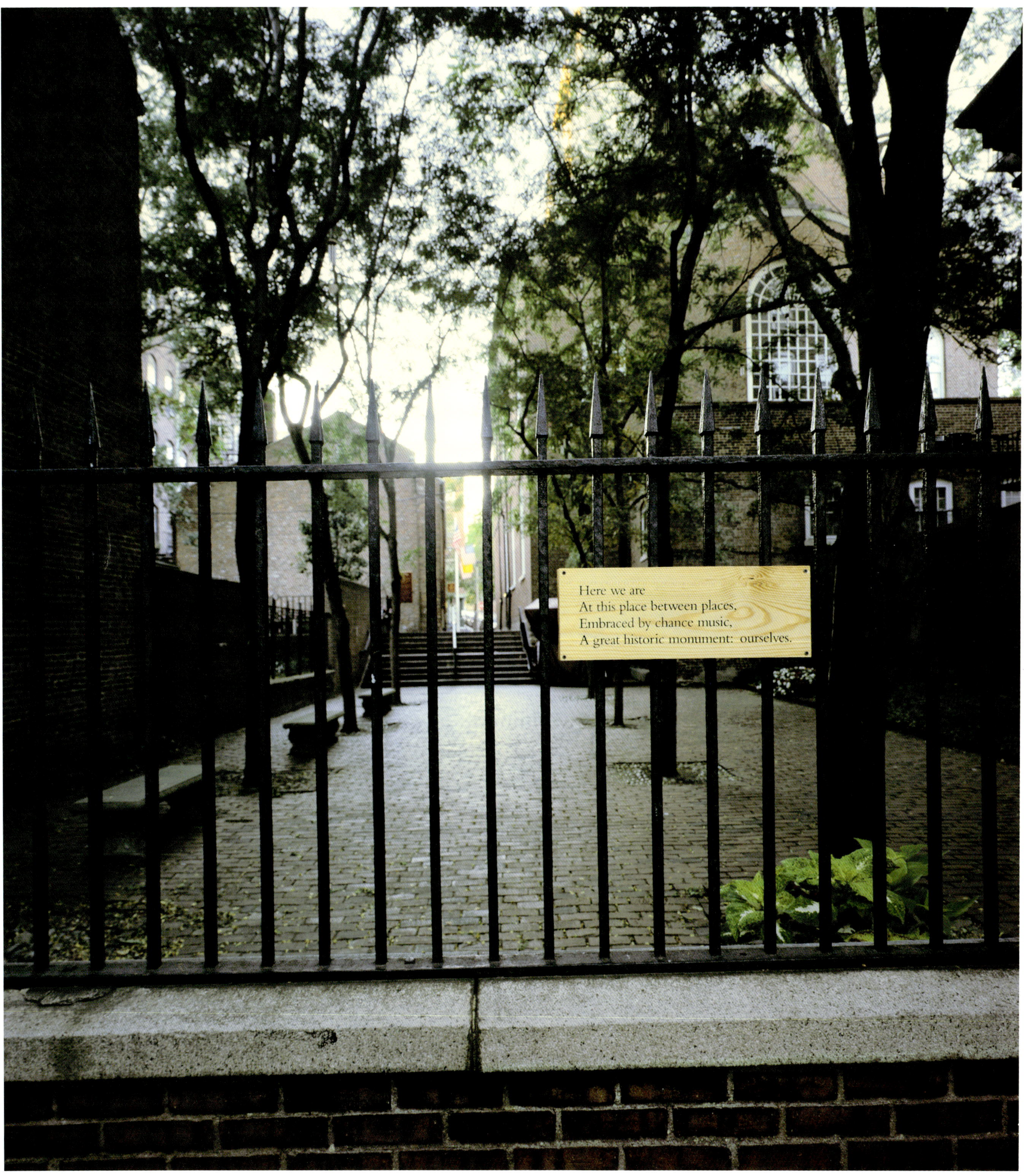
Here we are
At this place between places,
Embraced by chance music,
A great historic monument: ourselves.

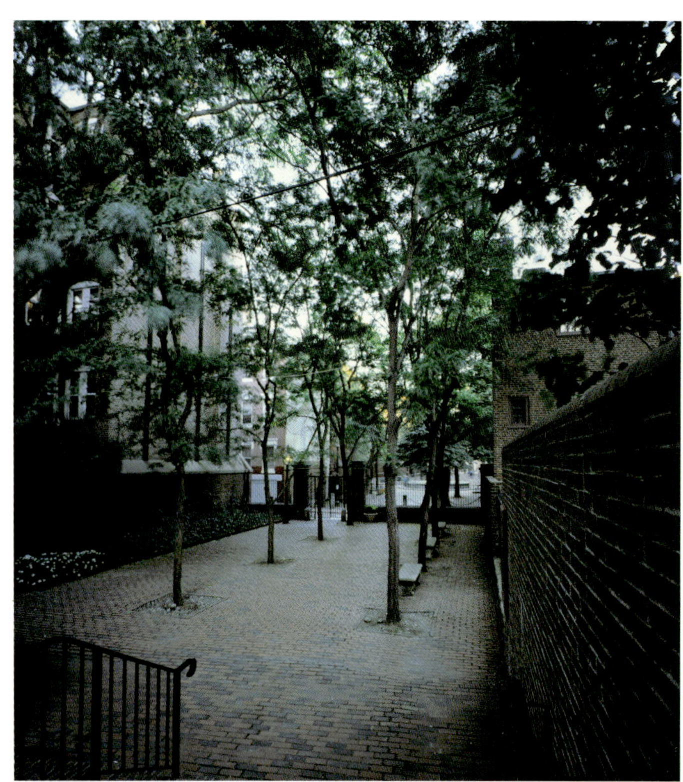

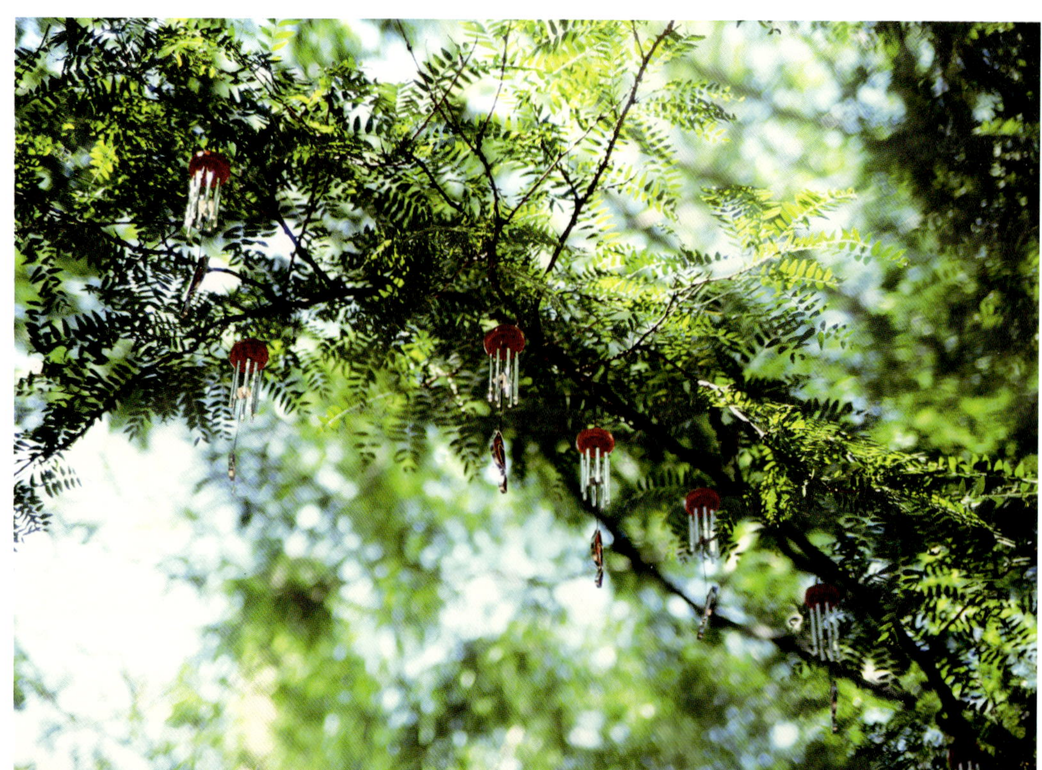

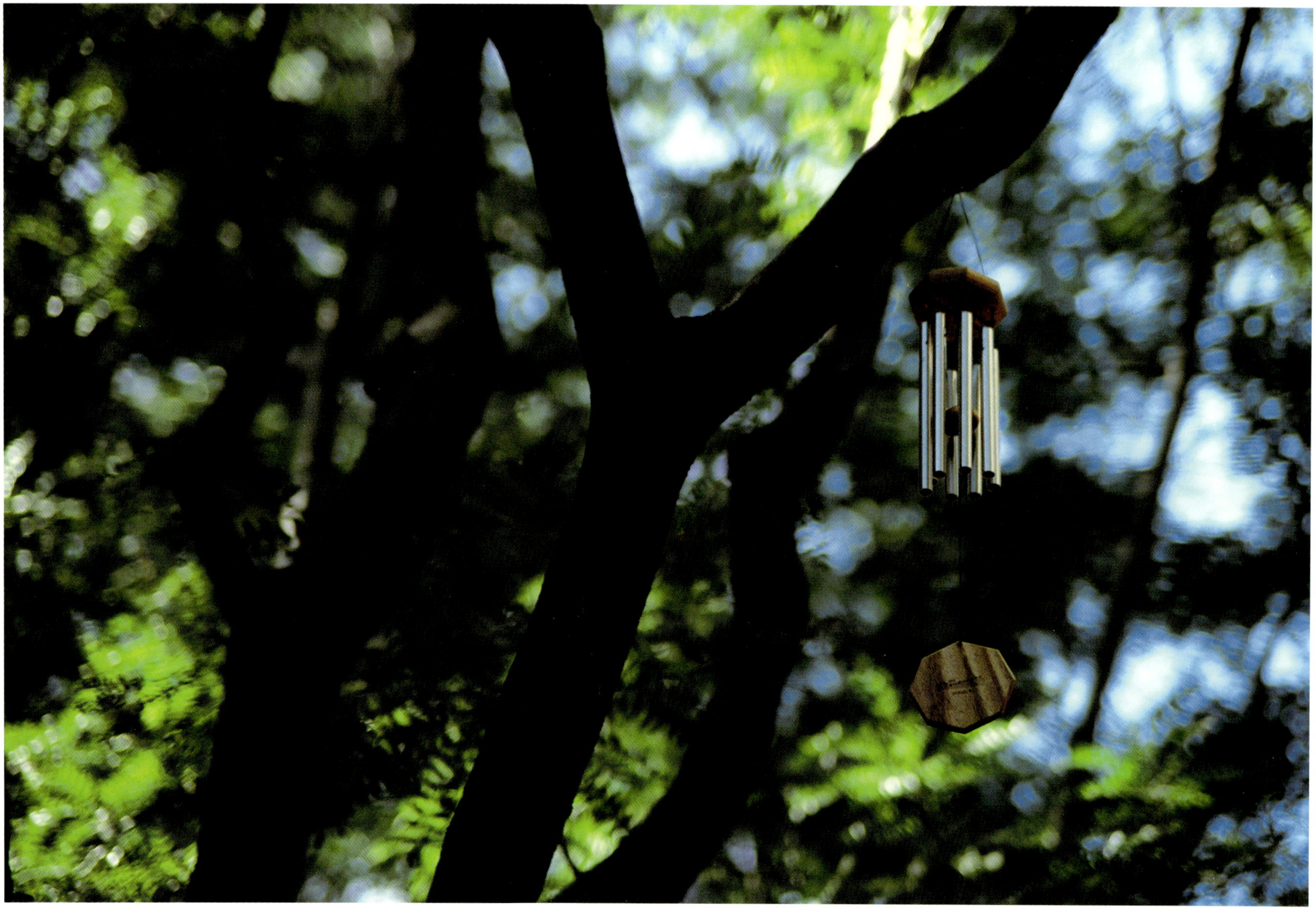

work to be hard to grasp or to contain physically, even. The piece resisted the framework of what was there, and required the interaction of nature with the chimes, and, of course, the chance that people would be there.

C.A.M. – Did it occur to you right away that wind chimes were the solution here?

J.H. – Yes, but I had to think carefully about how to use them. One time before I hung chimes in a garden in Venice. I made a wall of wind chimes, so it hung like a curtain. But I didn't like the way that it was so much about the objects, even though it evoked the idea of "wall of sound" or "curtain of sound." I thought that the weakness within that installation was my use of the instruments, the sound devices themselves, as objects. For *Here We Are* it was a deliberate choice to put the chimes high up in the trees, not emphasizing them as visual objects.

C.A.M. – There seemed to be a shift in your thinking about what types of chimes to use. At first you were going to have all kinds of chimes from all over. Then you decided to fabricate special ones for the project, which gave a nice, at least for me, visual unity to the piece. Those sweet little chimes complemented the leaves of the trees very well.

J.H. – I did want to get a variety of sound. But we were concerned about the piece being too loud or disruptive for people living close by. So I went for a chime that would make a softer sound.

C.A.M. – We did talk about that kind of logistical issue. But after the piece was up friends of mine who live in the area said they started to notice wind chimes everywhere in the neighborhood.

J.H. – That is funny.

C.A.M. – Would you talk some about how the plaque and poem complement the wind chimes?

J.H. – I don't know how clear the connection was. In fact, it was as if there were two pieces, although the words I used on it, "Here we are, at this place between places," were an important jumping off point for the whole project. I was also very interested in how there were so many commemorative plaques in the courtyard. I wanted to make a reference to some kind of historic event. I do believe we carry within ourselves historic events. We are all a part of nature, and history, too. It is interesting to talk about this stuff right now, with so many peace demonstrations happening.

C.A.M. – Yes. Someone decides that events and the people who played a role in them are important enough for the placement of a memorial or commemorative plaque. But what people are going to take away or bring to the situation will not be the official story, but their own stories and memories. It seems as though your impulse behind *Here We Are* honors this reality.

J.H. – In almost a subliminal way I was trying to affect collective memory, to create an association with sound and a particular space. In my day-to-day experience, I pass strangers and then pick up a certain note or hear a song or just feel a sensation. This then blends with the story going on in my head. And then part of my story becomes part of their story. These exchanges can become a framework for a particular event that is happening.

C.A.M. – You have talked about *Here We Are* as being a drawing in space. It seems the various interactions with it, chance or otherwise, are what make this drawing happen, or are what complete the work.

J.H. – Yes. The association of sound with a place can be very meaningful. Maybe one would be passing through that space, maybe with his or her child, and there is the sound of bells ringing. The mother hears the bell, and makes reference to it, or the child does. It becomes a shared experience and creates a memory that perhaps years down the line someone will say, "Do you remember when we had that day?" These are just shots in the dark, but the experience of not really knowing is becoming more and more important for me as time goes on. I continually try to keep myself in that kind of dark place, not in the sense of hopelessness, but more about the idea of wandering without really knowing.

C.A.M. – So that you remain open?

J.H. – Yes, open to experience.

Conversation between Mildred Howard and Carole Anne Meehan about *S.S.*, Let Freedom Ring, Inaugural ICA/Vita Brevis Project

Carole Anne Meehan – Would you talk a little about your first encounters with historic Boston?

Mildred Howard –When I walked the Freedom Trail I became aware that Boston has so much historical richness to it. I didn't know what to do at first. There seemed to be so many spaces to choose from.

C.A.M. –How did you settle on the Old South Meeting House?

M.H. – I was engaged by its history. Suffrage had begun there. Phyllis Wheatley, the first African American woman to publish her writing, attended services at Old South. The planning of the Boston Tea Party and the beginnings of Free Speech happened there. Abolitionists attended that church. I think these things, combined with what I already knew, were the turning point for me in deciding to use that space.

C.A.M. – How did you come to create a work with such a strong metaphoric reference to the Undergound Railroad?

M.H. – The phenomenon of the Underground Railroad is a metaphor for so many things. I have spent my life addressing issues around what it is to be an African American. In my work I explore the feelings and experiences common to everyone, including hopes, desires, and the boundaries of private and public. All of these kinds of things help me to develop a visual vocabulary to work from.

C.A.M. – What is meant by S.S.?

M.H. – S.S. was an abbrevation for "Slave Stealer." Many who were involved with Abolition were branded with this.

C.A.M. – Your ongoing themes of congregation and movement resonate beautifully in this piece. We know that the Underground Railroad wasn't a literal railroad but resulted in the movement of a community.

M.H. – Movement in community. Movement in thoughts. It is the commingling of these aspects that interests me. We are all a part of it. This whole Underground Railroad phenomenon wasn't just about African America.

C.A.M. – What kind of experience did you want to create for the viewer with the installation?

M.H. – Well, I wanted to create a sanctuary. It was made this way so that it would create a pure space in which to contemplate the past and present. Such as, when African Americans reached the North, there were still many other issues to deal with, even though now they were free Blacks. And many related issues persist to this day that affect not just Blacks, but so many of us, including other people of color, women, people who are gay and lesbian. There are so many rights that I feel my family worked for, that my ancestors and friends fought for, that are in the process of being overturned. It is just that I don't want these struggles ever to be forgotten.

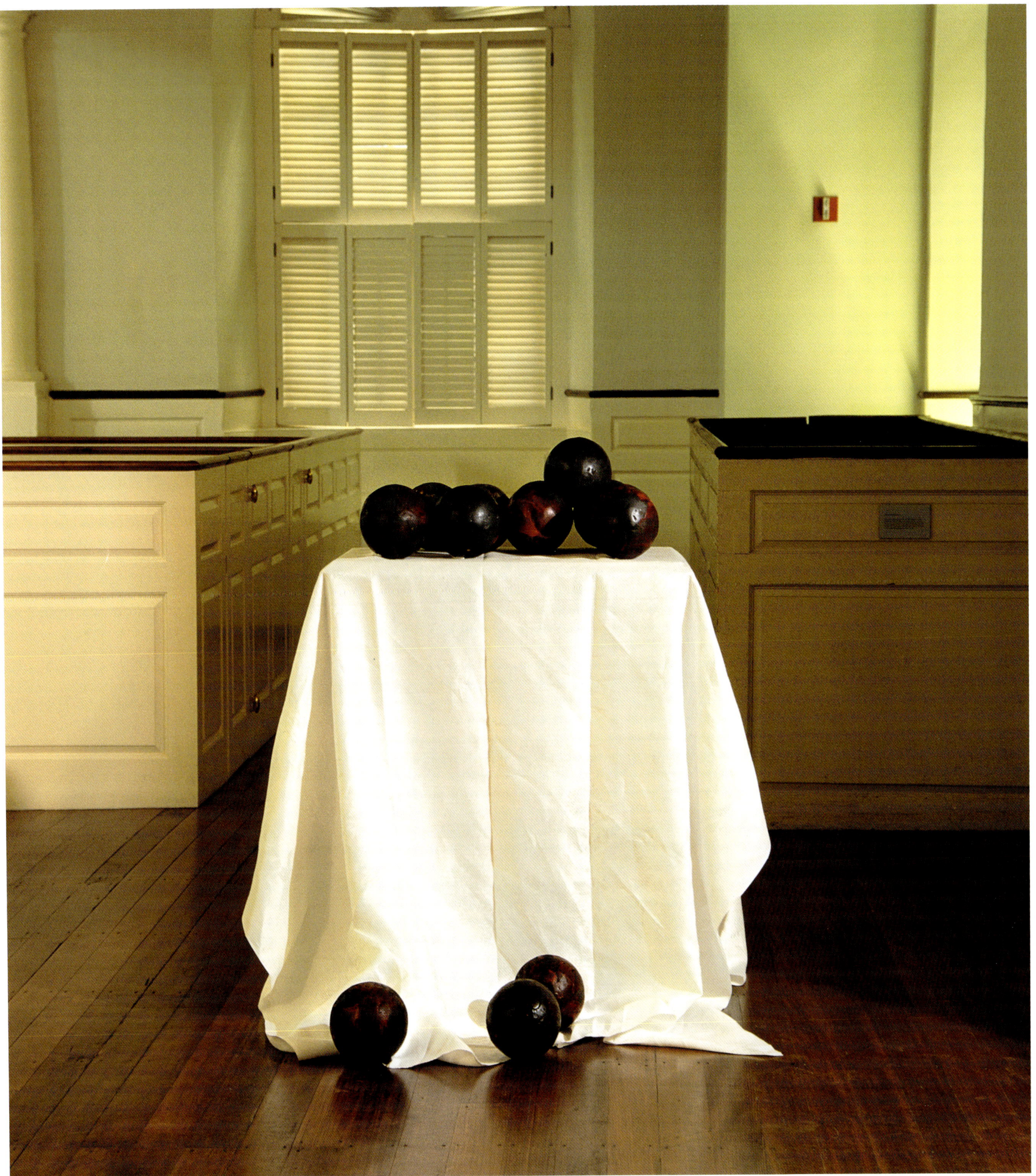

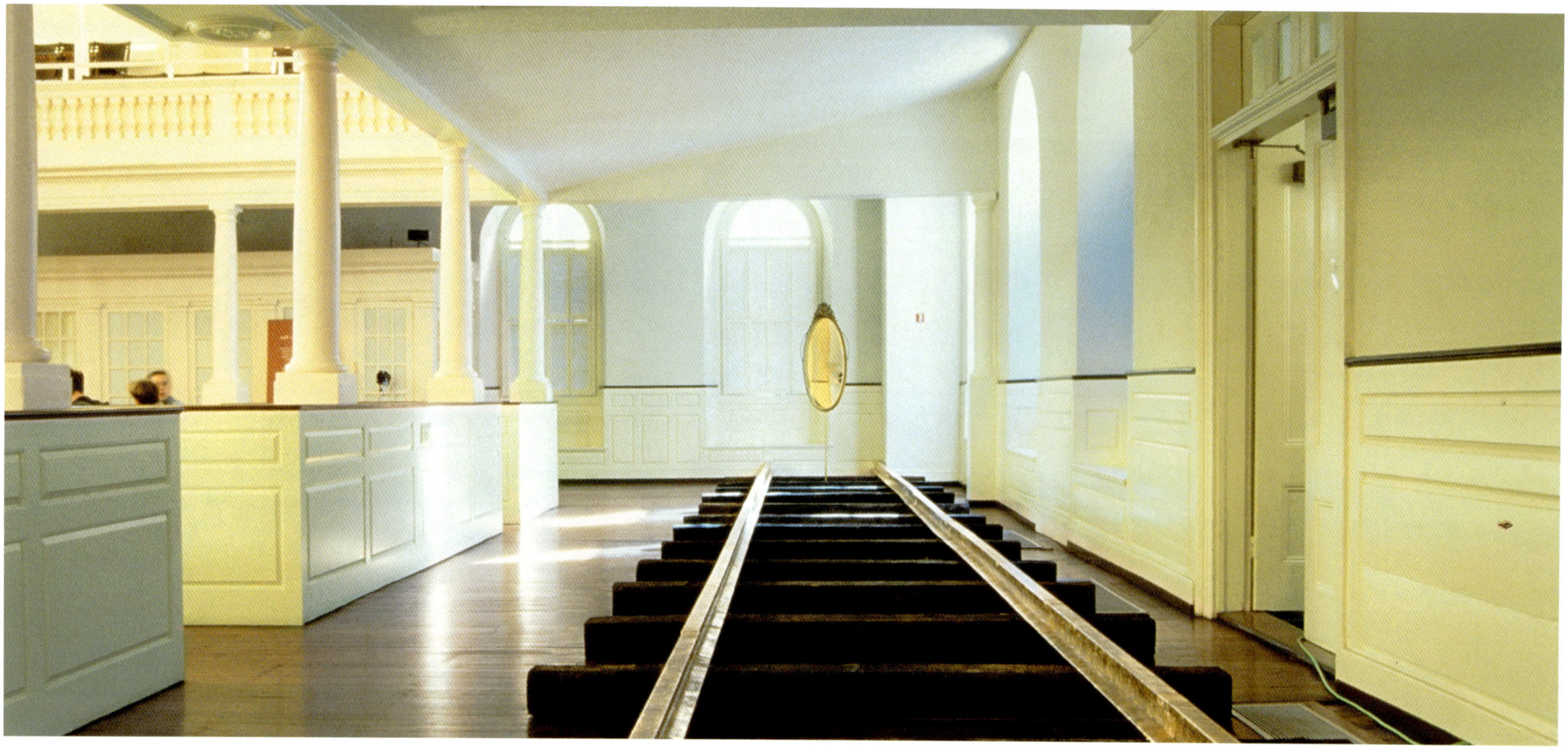

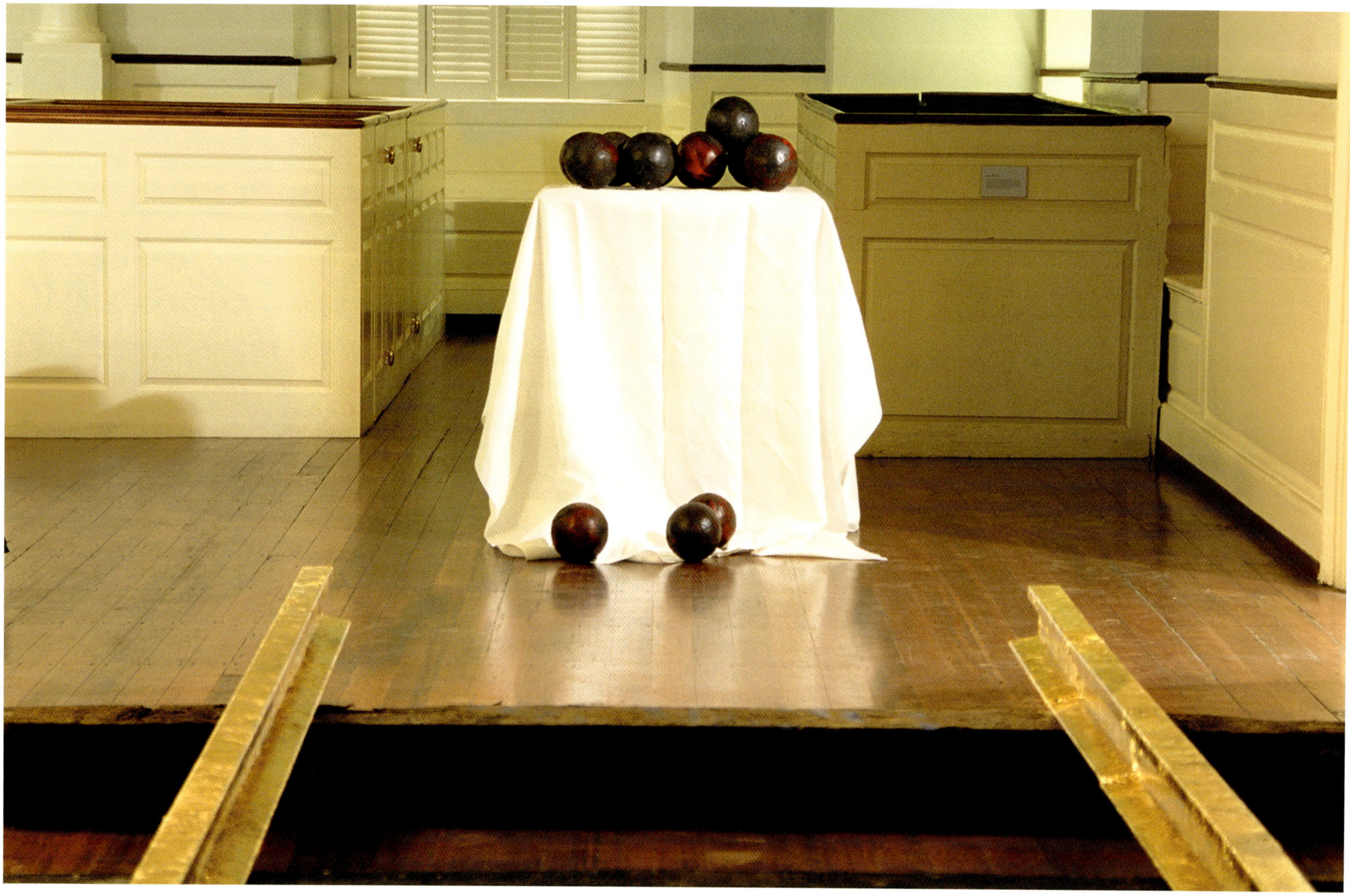

C.A.M. – So the state of the present day also informs the work.

M.H. – The then and the now are always present in my work. It is like blending the past and the present, creating a gray, inbetween area. I think about who we are as a country, not just who am I as Mildred, the African American. I am interested in how we got to where we are right now as a nation and how not to repeat the mistakes and atrocities of the past.

C.A.M. – It is interesting. You made this pristine sanctuary, but messy, bloody struggle is what you want the viewer to be aware of.

M.H. – Yes. Also, I wanted to evoke religion in the piece. So many wars have been fought over religion. But they have also been fought over oil, sugar, those things in life that all of us are so dependent on. So it is very much about control. You know, who has the most-est? (Laughs.) I never understood how one person or one group or one country thinks of themselves as more than another. How do people get that way and feel as though they can take a whole group of people and enslave them? I mean, think of the millions of people who died in the Middle Passage.

C.A.M. – Why did you put gold leaf on the railroad tracks?

M.H. – I wanted the tracks to refer to the route to the land of milk and honey.

C.A.M. – They are beautiful and appealing, but maybe another reading could be that the guilding refers to a certain kind of gaudiness, or coveting of worldly goods.

M.H. – Oh yes. We need to look at the fact that people lose their lives and land because of greed and ask, "OK, how can we do things differently?" Art can provide the big "what if?"

C.A.M. – Related to that point, you often talk about the uncertain future, and how the past is necessary to remember in order to root yourself in the present. Does this relate to your motivation for the use of the large mirror in the project?

M.H. – The mirror puts you right in the piece. It makes you look at yourself and then see how you fit into this whole picture. It is the opening of a domain for a perceptual experience that is not tied to any specifics. It could be the metaphor for so many things.

C.A.M. – So, in a sense, it has a neutrality?

M.H. – Well, it is a type of blank slate. Take a hard look in the mirror. It really all starts with each individual, each of whom has the potential to buy into this belief in our ability to transform the way we do things. It starts with each individual, and then it flows into collective experience. Art creates models of the world. It helps you develop ways of thinking that are different from the norm. It is just so wonderful to be able to be in that moment of developing other ways of thinking and not being afraid of doing that.

C.A.M. – It seems to me that all of that possibility frightens a lot of people.

M.H. – Fear is not really a good thing. It really isn't, but I think it is OK to feel a certain amount of loss of equilibrium. That is when you know something is shifting. That is when learning happens.

C.A.M. – Those moments are both unwelcome and welcome. One thing that is consistent throughout your work is an incredible sense of love, or an optimism, possibly bordering on patriotism. Your depictions of injustices, both on collective and personal levels, are not alienating. There is not a sense of "Well, to hell with it all."

M.H. – I love life. (Laughs.)

C.A.M. – That is very clear.

M.H. – I don't always like what life presents me with, but I still love it.

Conversation between Barbara Steinman and Carole Anne Meehan about *Colonnade*, Let Freedom Ring, Inaugural ICA/Vita Brevis Project

Carole Anne Meehan – You seem to be drawn to circular forms. Did your inspiration for *Colonnade* begin with the elegant circular structure of the Parkman Bandstand?

Barbara Steinman – Many of my sculptural works are circular and my time-based audio and video pieces are looped. I find that round rooms and circular structures evoke continuity. I was drawn to the Parkman Bandstand because of this quality and also because it appeared sculptural and sheltering within the open spaces of the park. Its period style made it look frozen in time and it already spoke of the past, a little like a monument.

C.A.M. – Speaking of monuments, the memorial statuary and plaques on the Boston Common became very important in the development of the piece.

B.S. – Once I had chosen the bandstand as a site, I explored the Boston Common to get to know its context. I was struck by the number of plaques and statuary commemorating victory and valorizing war. Thinking about the theme of the exhibition made me aware of the apparent relationships between war, sacrifice, and freedom based on the narratives on the plaques.

C.A.M. – Do you think of *Colonnade* as a memorial?

B.S. – Yes, I do, perhaps as a memorial to the idea of safeguarding freedom. I wanted to create a kind of soft memorial site.

C.A.M. – What do you mean by "soft" memorial?

B.S. – A "soft" memorial could be dedicated to convictions or ideas as well as commemorate a specific event. It could incorporate elements designed to resonate or change over time. It could even express doubt or be inconclusive. It most likely would be unconcerned with high visibility or permanence, and would allow for an unpredictable future. It might incorporate "live" elements, such as a garden or a piece of music played every year on a certain date. It might be made of light and appear only at night. In these ways artists are able to question traditional ideas about the forms of expression that are right for "remembering" in the public sphere.

C.A.M. – Speaking of light, this was an important element in *Colonnade*. Would you talk some about your use of light in the work?

B.S. – At night, the bandstand was so brightly lit from within it was like both a beacon and a contained space from which to look out at the Boston Common, a place that feels far from safe to me, particularly at night. The need for the piece to feel sheltering was very important since feeling safe is an aspect of freedom. So *Colonnade*'s design called for illuminating the fabric banners that hovered in front of the bandstand's columns, making them glow at night.

C.A.M. – Speaking of the banners, was creating the poem that you put on them an enjoyable or painstaking process?

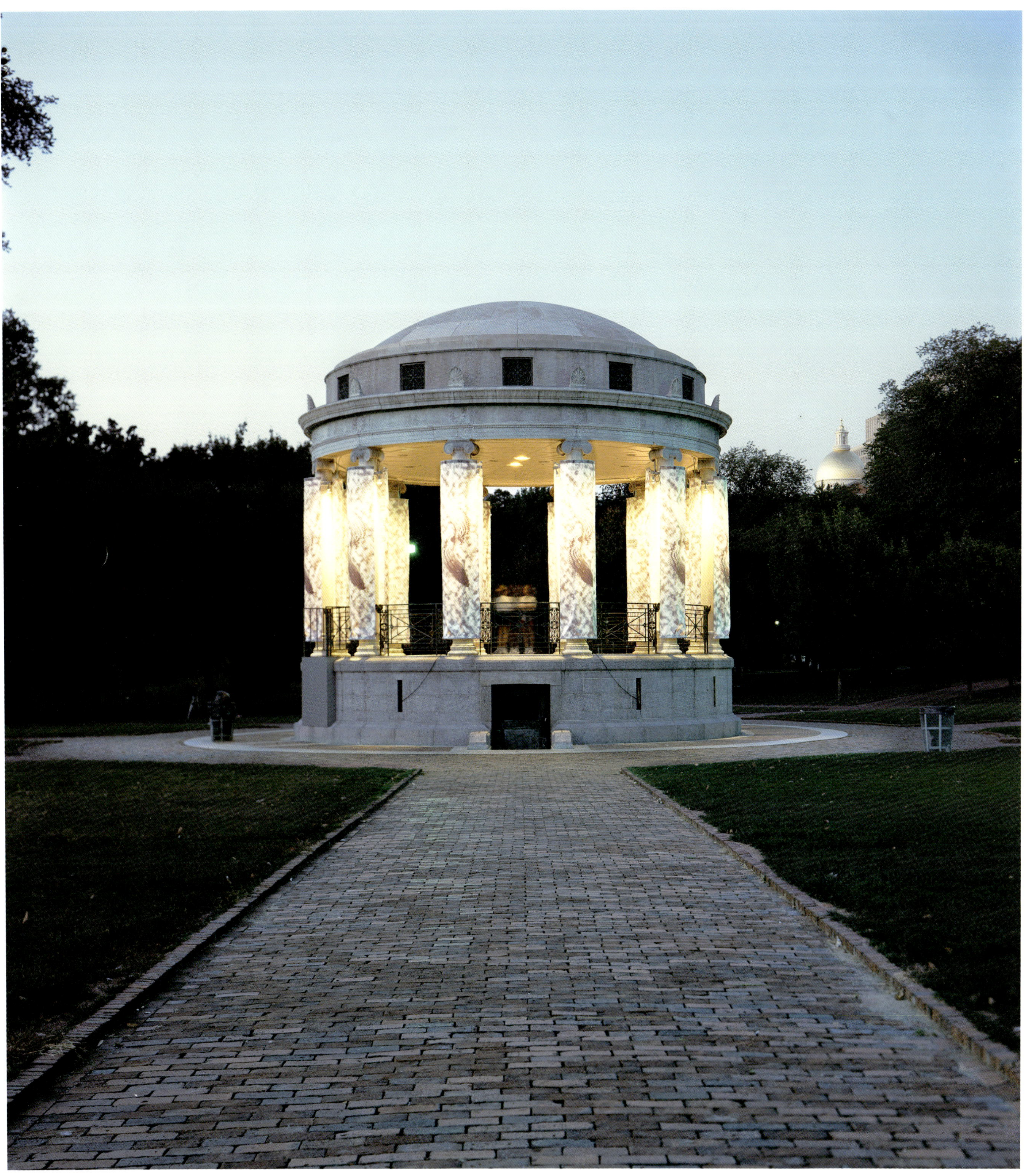

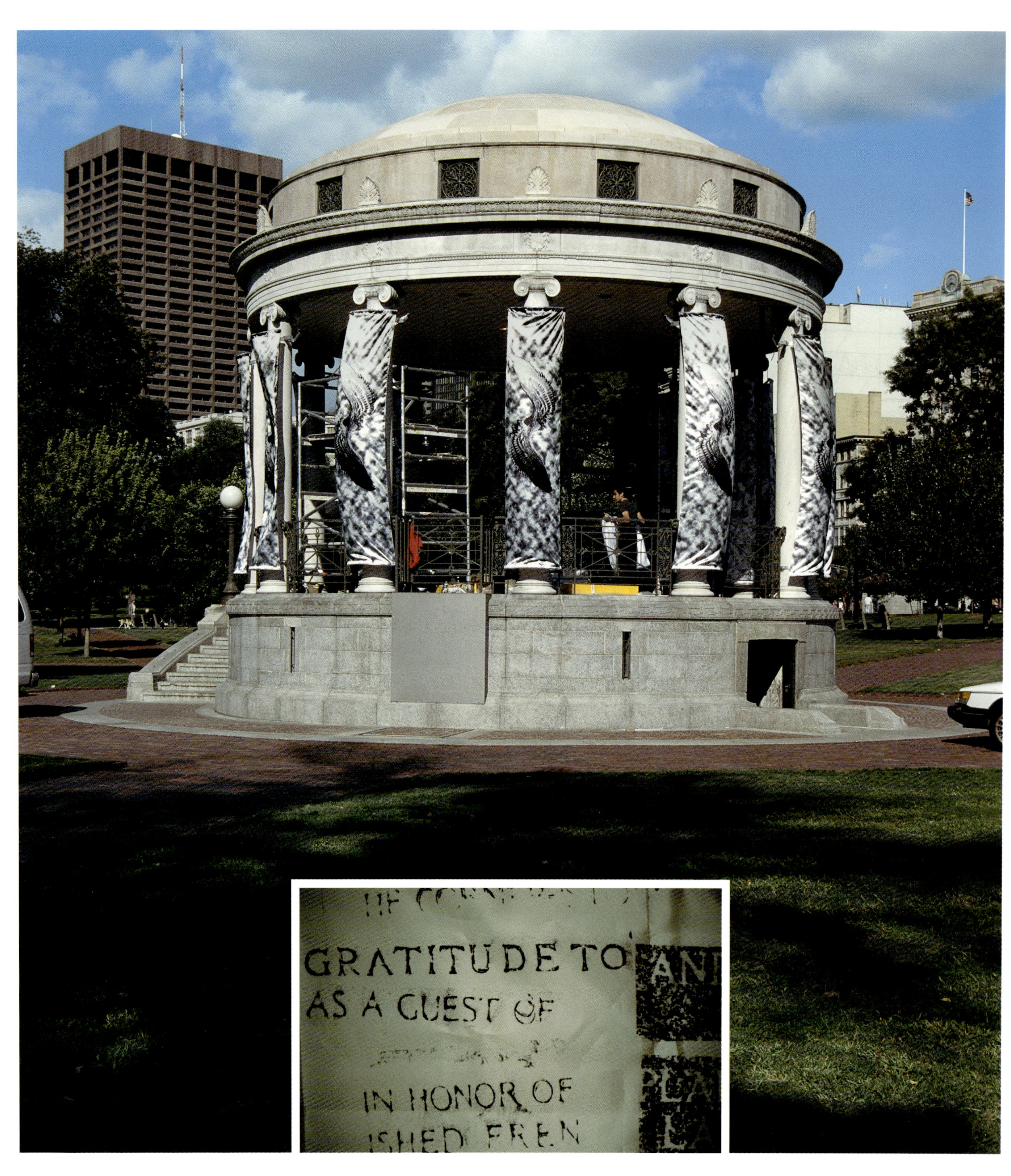
GRATITUDE TO
AS A GUEST OF
IN HONOR OF

B.S. – Shuffling and playing with the words and phrases gathered from the Common was very enjoyable. I wanted to extract words that appealed to me, and that would tell a story other than war and massacre. Living in Montreal, a predominantly French-speaking city, makes one very aware of language, translation, and meanings that lie between languages. Looking for fragments of text and rearranging them may come out of my experience of continuously shifting between languages.

C.A.M. – What about the bandstand's original purpose as a small concert pavilion? What were your impressions of its acoustic properties?

B.S. – The acoustic properties of the bandstand were special. Memorials are usually silent, but here the sound of the wind was amplified to such an extent that a breeze could sound like a gale. Bits of conversations floated through, fragmented like the words on the panels.

C.A.M. – Have you had any new thoughts about the project five years later?

B.S. – I chose the bandstand, a concert stage, as a neutral and benign site. Knowing more now about places in the world where female voices are suppressed, where girls and women do not have the freedom to sing or play music, the bandstand would be a less neutral site for me.

C.A.M. – The poem is about an alternative way of looking at safeguarding freedom. Would you be willing to share any thoughts you may have about the various approaches to safeguarding freedom that are now being experimented with?

B.S. – So many of the commemorative plaques on the Boston Common tell of the necessity of battle, sacrifice, and war in order to uphold freedom. In 1998 the histories contained within the monuments seemed far away, remote. But now the themes of Let Freedom Ring feel more urgent. Freedom seemed like a given in America at that moment in 1998, though, to me, freedom is always a fragile possibility. The reworked text that I used in *Colonnade* feels cautionary then as now.

Conversation between Krzysztof Wodiczko and Carole Anne Meehan about *The Bunker Hill Monument Projection*, Let Freedom Ring, Inaugural ICA/Vita Brevis Project

Carole Anne Meehan – How did you come to choose the Bunker Hill Monument for your project?

Krzysztof Wodiczko – I made my choice in part by thinking about the mission of the project, which was called Let Freedom Ring. The monument is at the end of the Freedom Trail, its grand finale and a landmark known to the city. It was hard to say no to such a structure. At the beginning I was sufficiently informed to know that the monument is implicated in the continuation of some battle over liberty.

C.A.M. – Do you mean a contemporary battle as opposed to the Revolutionary era?

K.W. – Yes. The pursuit of happiness, justice for all and, most importantly, life. With my work I am not trying to actualize the past, but to see to what degree the past has anticipated the present. This was a place that was not selected on the basis of the past but on the basis of what I overheard in my initial investigation about the situation in Charlestown involving its high rate of unsolved murders. I did know something about it, but I didn't want to start from the immediate problems around it. I wanted to make sure that I explored the wider situation in the city, knowing that the monument overlooks the whole city of Boston and can hear and see troubles everywhere.

C.A.M. – But yet you ended up working with some key members of the immediate community of Charlestown.

K.W. – I was always thinking that the project would arise from specific groups and inhabitants whose experience needs to be transmitted to the entire city and maybe to the whole United States, and to some degree the world, eventually. There would be a link between their specific problems and the problems that other people have elsewhere, so that it would be a truly public project. In other words, I wanted to use the monument to transmit messages that are of vital importance to everybody. In this way the Charlestown situation became more global, and a concentration of some trouble that happens everywhere.

C.A.M. – The presence of the symbol of American independence right in the center of the neighborhood, which is only one square mile in size, seemed so poetically odd in that many members of the community seemed to be against the exercising of one's right to speak freely.

K.W. – Yes, in the United States Constitution the right to expression is the first right. In the French Constitution this liberty holds the seventh position. In Charlestown some members of the community impose limitations on themselves with regard to this right. This must be the result of some terror or domination by the few over the many. The silence is a way of life, otherwise you may lose your life.

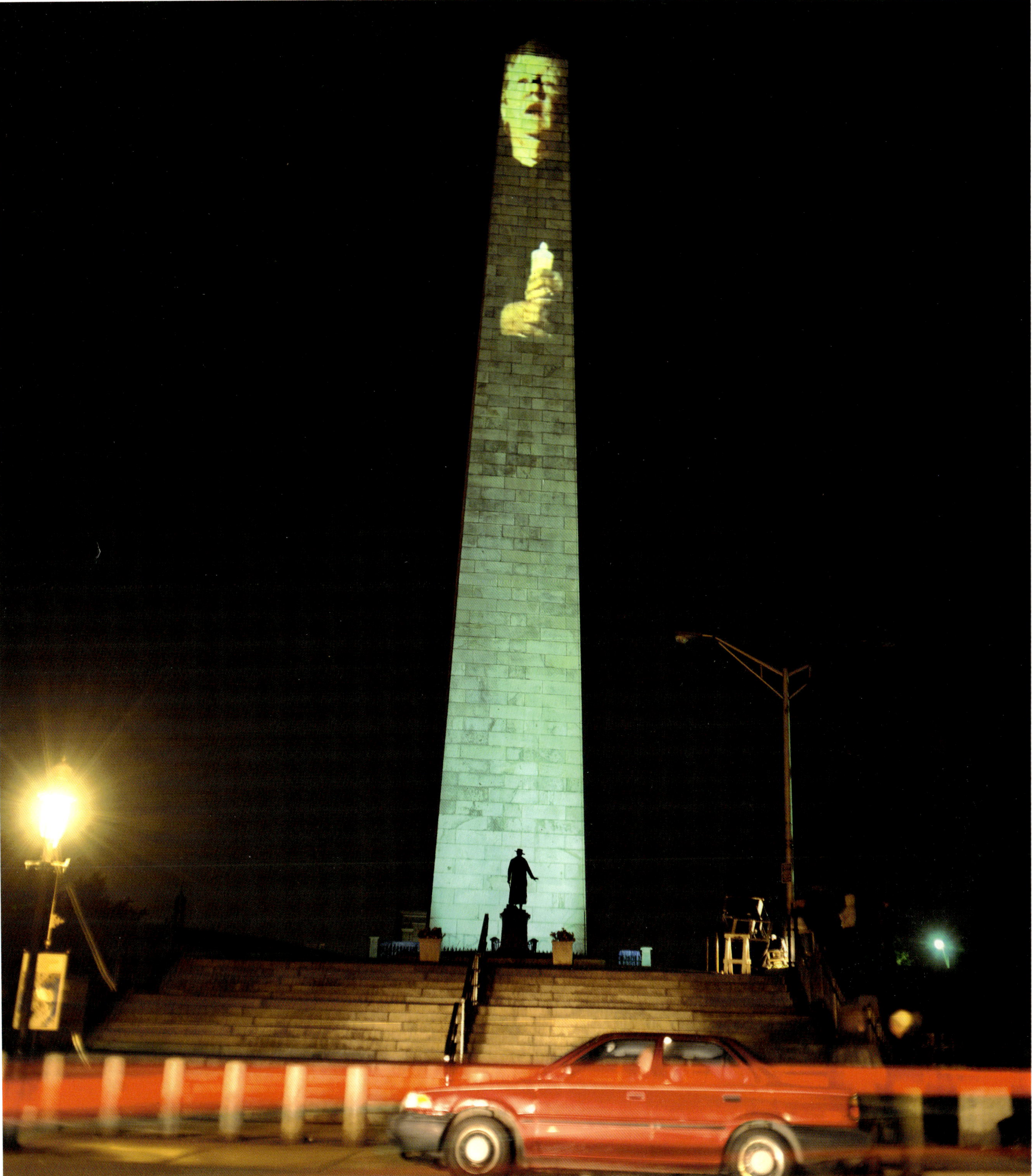

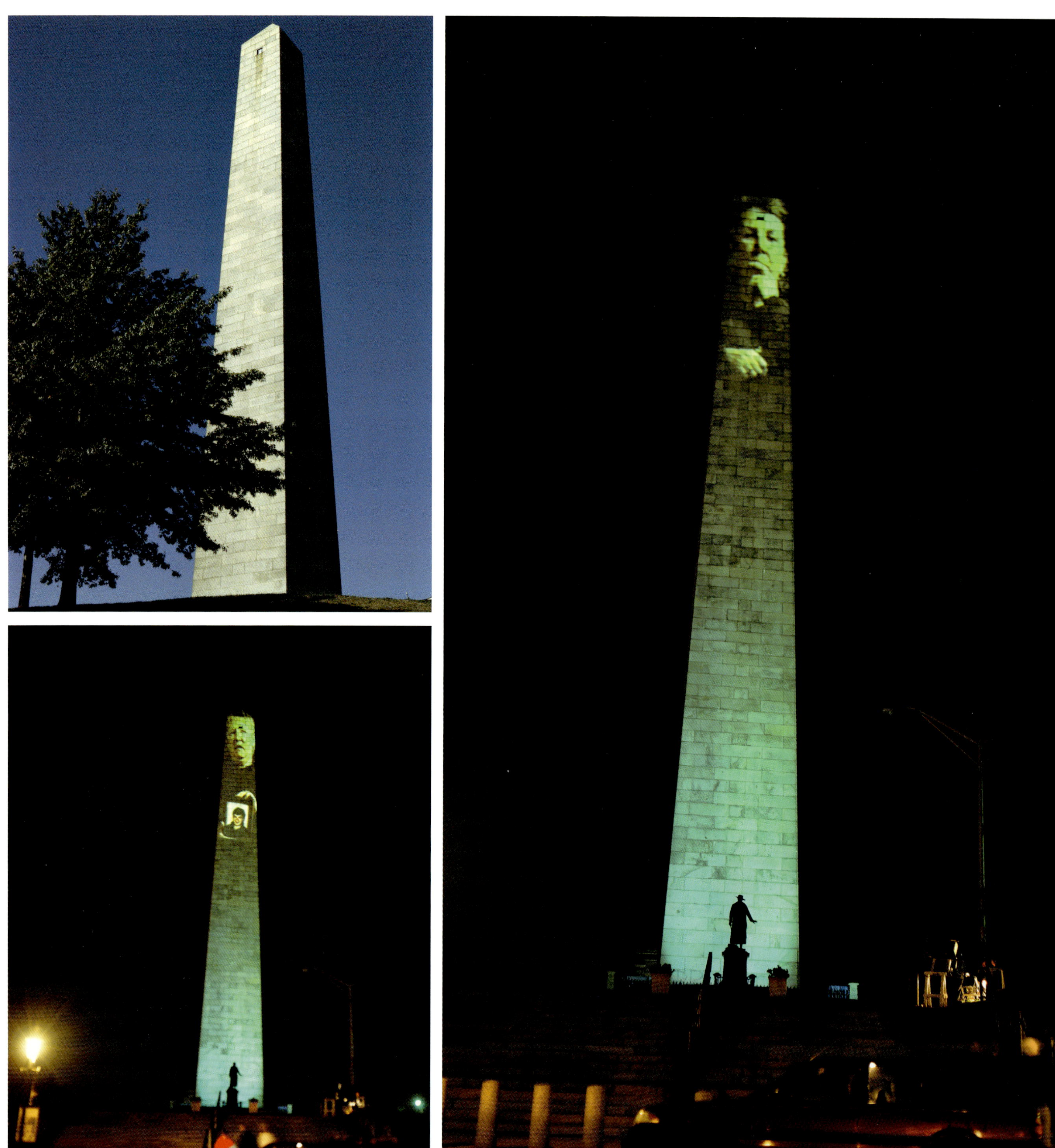

C.A.M. – Can you speak some more about how you arrived at projecting the voices and faces of Charlestown residents at the top of the monument?

K.W. – At one point someone who was considering participating in this project asked, "What if the monument could speak?" The conversation turned toward how the monument had heard and seen a lot. This became an actual metaphor, because there is an incredible intimacy between the monument and life in Charlestown. The monument was built in the center of this very densely populated area. It is seen from everywhere and, in turn, it is seeing everything. Every time someone is shot or wounded, it becomes a witness to what is happening. The monument hears and remembers it all.

C.A.M. – The grounds around the monument make up one of the only open green spaces in the neighborhood. It is an important recreational area for the community.

K.W. – I am sure there is plenty of playing and resting and eating that goes on there, but some shootings took place in the park. The monument becomes a family member of those who remember these events as they grow older. Also, in this sense, those who suffered the devastating loss identify with the monument. The tragedy of losing one's child becomes the defining event, the center, so to speak, of your universe. It is the most unspeakable tragedy so one becomes, in a way, a monument, too.

C.A.M. – What about your interaction with the mothers? It seemed they were up to the difficult task of participating in the project because they had been working so diligently on their grief around losing their kids to urban violence, both publicly and privately, for years before we met them. They were activists, involved in both self-healing and community healing. In the *New York Times* you referred to them as "heroines of the democratic process."

K.W. – You have brought up several topics. We can start with addressing democracy in terms of the ancient Greek concept of the "fearless speaker." Certain individuals were identified to be the most qualified, and key, forces in the democratic process. The question that was asked was how should people be selected and educated to become speakers? And who should we value the most among these speakers? Such a speaker should have an image of self-esteem, but not selfishness. He should possess some force that drives him to tell the truth. And, he should not be concerned with personal safety, about keeping a job nor receiving an award. There is certainly something heroic about a person like this.

C.A.M. – This description of the "fearless speaker" sounds like a description of the mothers you worked with.

K.W. – Yes. Today we have people who are silent but who have a right to speak. But the members of this group were already speaking, which was part of their process of recovering from trauma. So there were fearless speakers right there in Charlestown. They were able to use my project for the further advancement of their message. They used it very well, as they have used effectively other forms of media. And because they have used media and are, as a result, recognized figures, they are more protected, because if anything happens to them, it would be the subject of an investigation on a large scale.

C.A.M. – What you say reminds me that you have often talked about the projections and also your instruments as being communication vehicles for the "other," for the stranger. What is interesting here is that the members of our group were anything but the other. They had been in Charlestown for generations. But as soon as they became victims they became the other in the eyes of their neighbors.

K.W. – Yes. And then they must be kept under surveillance because they might come to the conclusion that they have nothing to lose anymore, so they can start speaking. They ask themselves, "Why should I fear for my life? I have already lost everything that was most important to me." They testify against others without fearing retribution and also with a sense of mission.

C.A.M. – Can you talk more specifically about why they were such effective speakers for the project and in terms of your ideas in general?

K.W. – They realized that their overwhelming sense of trauma is unique, but not exclusive. They know there are other people who suffer and who have survived similar events. By speaking they help to transform the world. They become agents for change. This is possible only through having some distance from one's own trauma. This way you can extrapolate the very personal into a social or historical mission. So here the fearless speaker becomes both a patient and a doctor. Not very many people who have suffered trauma have arrived at this stage. That is why during the three evenings of the projection five or six mothers said to me they thought they would now be ready to be a part of the projection, and were sorry they couldn't earlier. Of course by then it was too late. But the point becomes not whether or not they participate, but that they came quickly to this conclusion. If they are ready to be a part of such a projection then they are ready to walk through the legal system, to break the code of silence, and to join those who really create a challenge to the culture. So, in this sense, the projection was very effective, even for those who didn't participate directly.

C.A.M. – The young man was an interesting addition to the voices of the three mothers in the projection.

K.W. – The young man was speaking on behalf of traumatized youth. He filled in that void made by the young men the mothers spoke of who were lost to the senseless killing.

C.A.M. – It would be interesting to talk more about how you and the group arrived at the decision to expose the face for this project.

K.W. – This became an act of defiance of the code of silence. It is true that I would not have considered showing their faces without their demanding it. They also insisted on showing photographs of the faces of their children, and some of their personal objects.

C.A.M. – Their insistence on this underscores again their incredible bravery. Did having to include their faces create any technical challenges?

K.W. – It was almost impossible to make a connection between their bodies and the "body" of the monument. It took an enormous amount of work during the editing process to make this connection look and feel natural, to make it look as though they had become themselves the height of the 221-foot obelisk. I needed to accept that it was not as perfect or as seamless as I would like.

C.A.M. – Maybe it wasn't seamless, but the final projection tape was very effective and convincing in making the monument look animated by their faces and voices.

K.W. – To do this we needed to film people from a very low, steep angle that would be approximately the same as the angle from which their images would be projected. In the studio we had to help them climb onto a pedestal, so, in a sense, they were already monuments in the studio. Now they see the world, or at least the studio, from the height of the monument. This is my adaptation of a technique used to help war veterans, the "helicopter technique," that gives victims the opportunity to view the sites of trauma from a heightened perspective. The whole theatricality and absurdity of this climbing disrupted the focus on their own tragedy and helped to create some distance. It became a semi-comical situation that allowed people to say something before bursting into tears.

C.A.M. – You mentioned the ancient notion of festival in connection with this project.

K.W. – This again relates to ancient practices of democracy. During the Greek festivals people from various cities that may have been in conflict with one another were granted special immunity so that they could be free to enter and participate in athletic and artistic competitions, such as the reciting of poetry and so forth. During these occasions spectators and participants would accept each other. They would treat each other as adversaries, but not enemies. In the case of Charlestown, during the three nights of the projection, you could see people observing this spectacle together who would normally not tolerate each other or accept each other's presence. This is the spirit of the festival. Also, the fact that the monument is owned and managed by the National Park Service made the projection very democratic in that the Park Service represents the larger society and a larger interest, actually including all of the United States. This was underscored by the comments of the Park Ranger who said that this artist must be crazy, but that he had the right to use the U.S.-owned property in this way.

C.A.M. – The public vigils organized by the mothers beginning in 1992, where their murdered children are remembered, also provide a place and a moment where adversaries are able to stand side by side in a contemporary truce. They have created a very democratic, healing tradition.

K.W. – It is good they do this on an ongoing basis. The ancient roots of democracy recognize the dynamic aspects of the democratic system. It is never really a completed project. It is a learning process.

Shimon Attie: *An Unusually Bad Lot*

The 2nd Annual ICA/Vita Brevis Project
December 1999

Conversation between Shimon Attie and Carole Anne Meehan
about *An Unusually Bad Lot,*
2nd Annual ICA/Vita Brevis Project

Carole Anne Meehan – What are some thoughts you have had since *An Unusually Bad Lot* was presented in 1999/2000?

Shimon Attie – The first thing that comes to mind is the way world events are going, in particular in the United States. One has more and more a sense of absolute astonishment and speechlessness. Should we laugh or cry? The issues that the project touched on are, in a sense, becoming more and more relevant to what is going on today.

C.A.M. – How are these issues more relevant?

S.A. – Think of the anti-immigrant content. Today immigrant equals terrorist. There is a lack of due process in the law. Basic civil liberties, especially in the judicial system, are eroding, such as detention without charges being filed, and so on. The murky way the judicial system deals with suspected terrorists today feels to me to be very similar to the kinds of accusations, assignations, condemnations, and so on, that we saw in the text of old police records that I used in *An Unusually Bad Lot.*

C.A.M. – Would you describe how you conceived of the project?

S.A. – It is difficult for any artist to articulate fully the creative process they go through in conceiving a project. It is perhaps like cooking a soup with many different ingredients. In my case it involved immersing myself in the site and history of the ICA's building, and also spending a great deal of time at the police archives poring over dozens of case files. Slowly, the idea of how to give visual form to the socially and politically charged history of the building came into focus.

C.A.M. – Would you elaborate some on how the building's charged history was compelling to you?

S.A. – I was intrigued by what I saw as its dual purpose, first as a former police precinct and detention center which then transformed into a contemporary art museum. I was interested in this confluence of criminology and culture, which seemed like a very rich arena to explore.

C.A.M. – What role did the building's architecture play in your development of the project?

S.A. – Its ornate frolic and curvilinear architectural motifs indeed did grab me. These elements seemed ripe for inscription with the unfolding laser projected handwriting we used and the interplay between that and the projected portraits. Also, its nineteenth-century design fit with the period I was mining for the project.

C.A.M. – Speaking of that, what was the experience of digging through all of those old police records like?

S.A. – It was largely one of both amazement and astonishment. Some of the accusations against these "bad" women and men were so horrific in their implicit racism, sexism, xenopho-

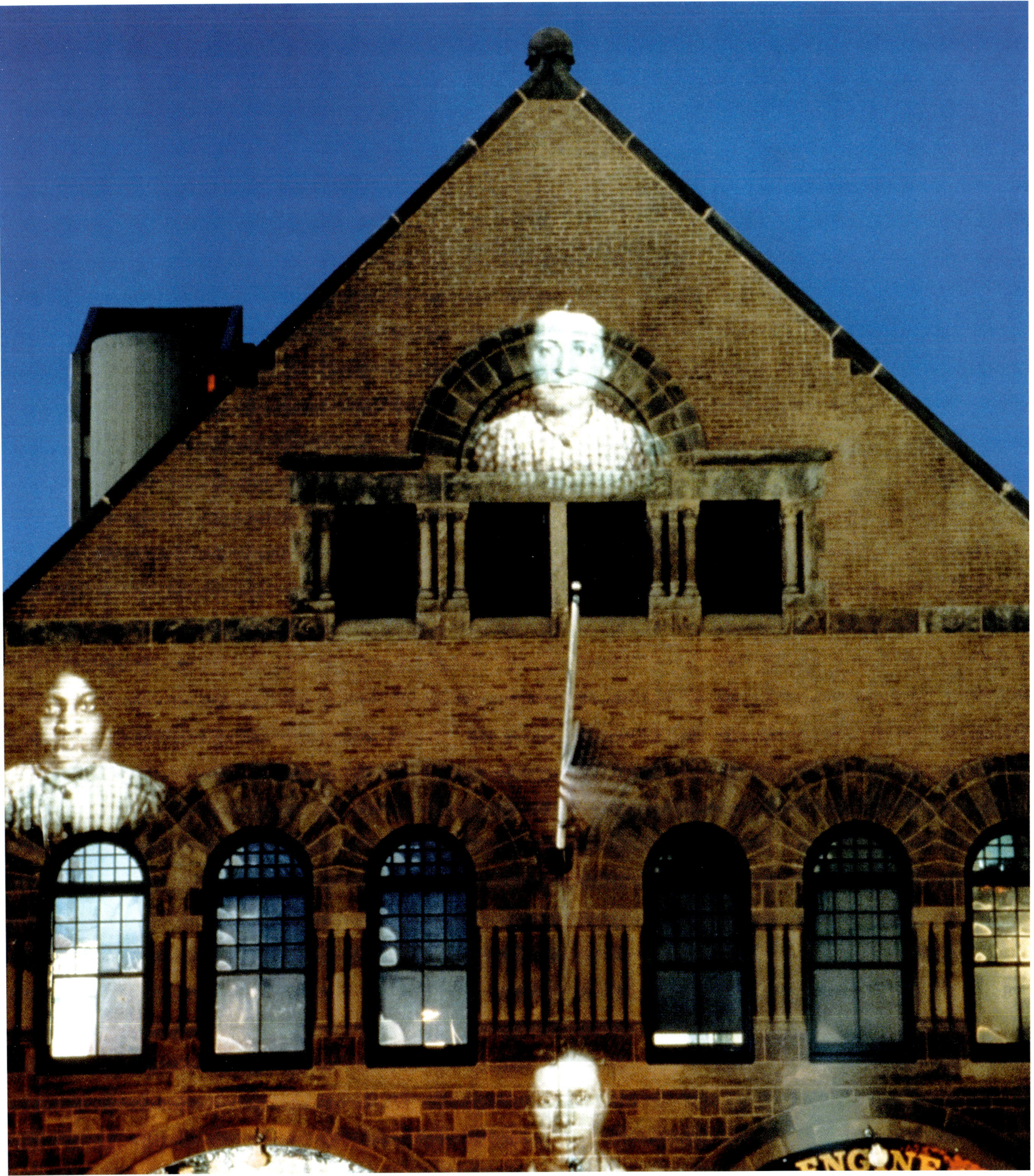

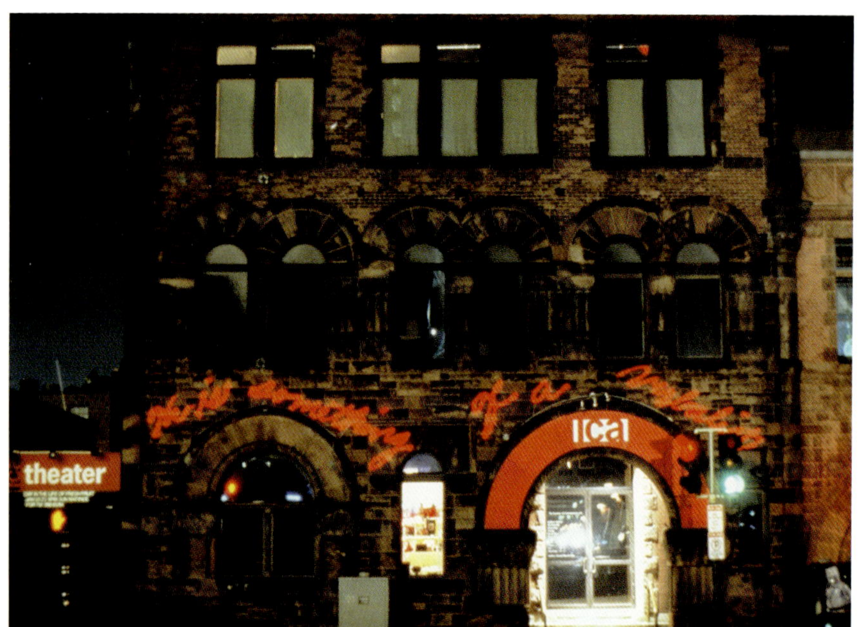
theater
ica

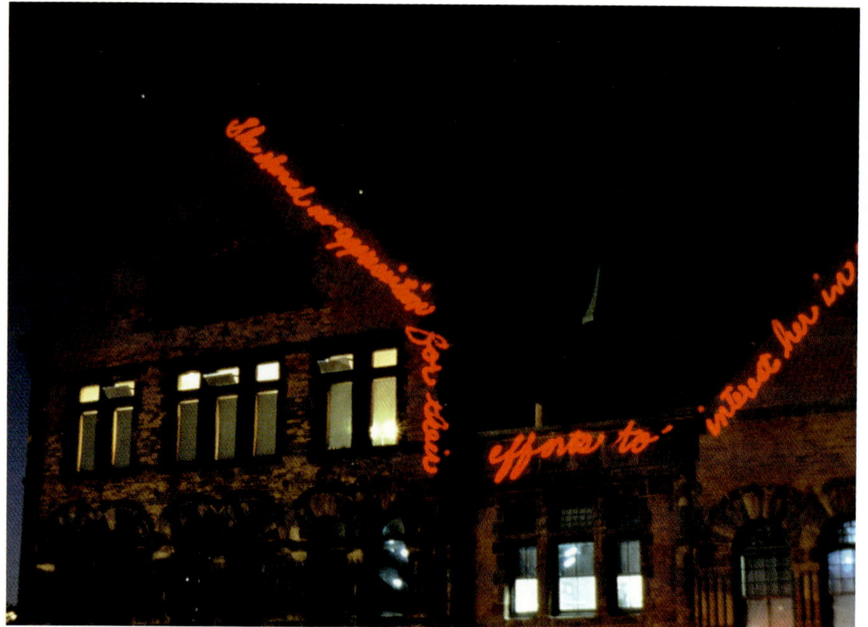

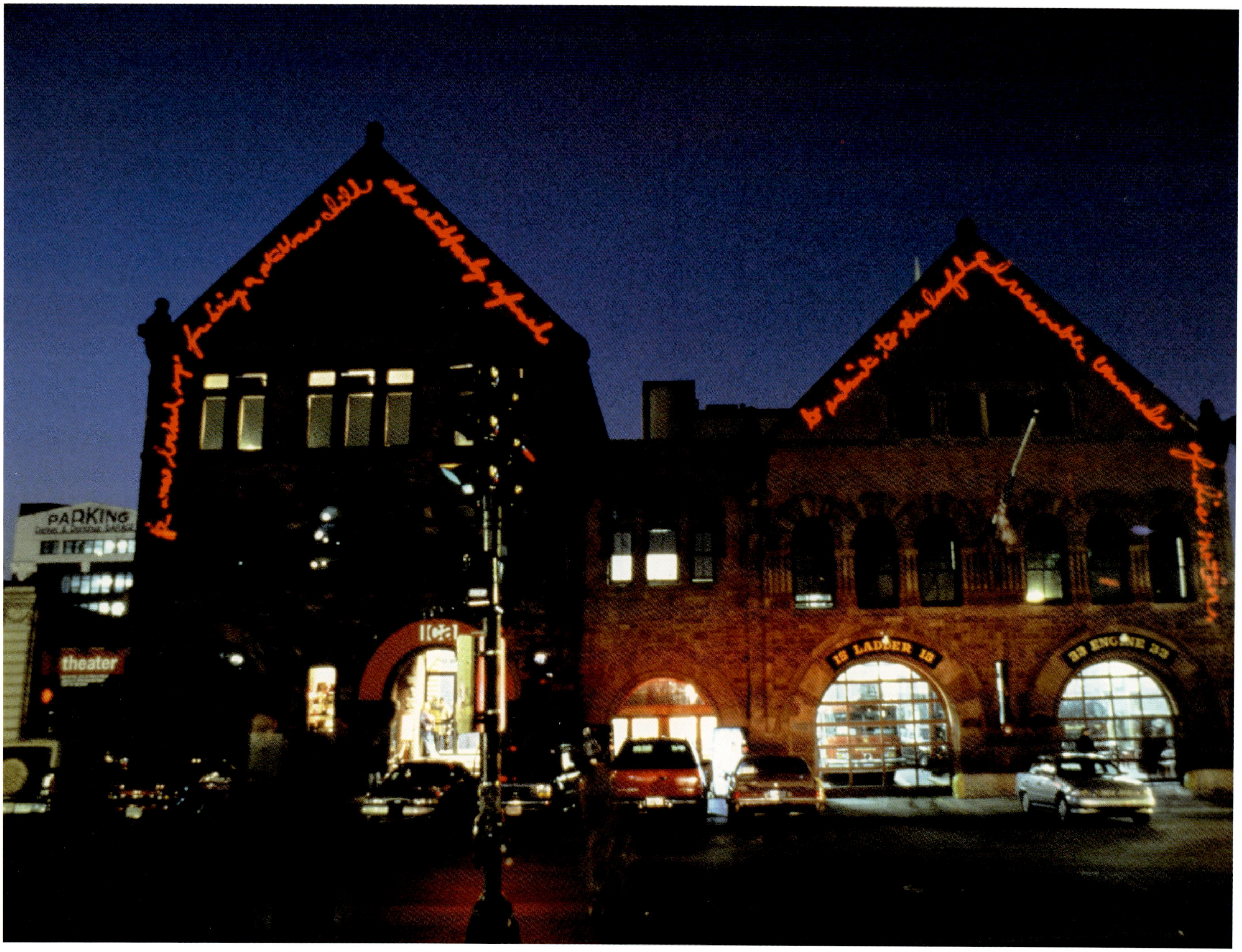

bia, and so on. Reading through the police reports I didn't know whether to cry, be angry or laugh. It was the tension between my different responses that created what could be called "counter-phobic" humor that I wanted to drive the tenor of the final artwork. It was also amazing to see how everyone was in on the condemnations of the accused, including his or her mother, stepfather, priest, family physician, police sergeant, and so on. It made me think of what the dynamic must have been like during the Salem witch trials.

C.A.M. – The use of language in these records was extremely important to the shape of the final artwork. Would you talk some about how you chose the language from these that would form the basis of the work's projection texts?

S.A. – What amazed me was the utter transparency and lack of self-consciousness of the language used in these reports. For example, consider the following excerpt, "She did not seem to feel ashamed being arrested for fornication, not even with a colored man." I wanted the texts to be concise distillations of the various issues that the project was engaging. By today's standards, many of them seem hyperbolic and colorful, and it was to these texts that I was most drawn. They conveyed the most using the least amount of words.

C.A.M. – Do you think you developed a sympathy with the people you encountered in these case files?

S.A. – I do, in fact. It is difficult to imagine the kind of pain and suffering these people went through, primarily because they simply refused to conform to the sexual and social mores of their time. I don't know how I myself would have fared under such conditions.

C.A.M. – It seems to me that the stories from a century ago that you uncovered in *An Unusually Bad Lot* are still unfolding. Recently the newspaper had a front-page story about a woman who has been accused of several bank robberies. The article, which is full of personal details, talks quite a bit about how rare is it for women to rob banks. This woman, whom the police refer to as "Bonnie," is not living according to the expectations of her gender. To quote from the story, "In police circles [she] stands out, not for her heroin use, but for bypassing the crimes female drug users typically turn to: shoplifting and prostitution." This newspaper story makes me wonder if there is anything different now. It is almost as though you didn't need to draw from late-nineteenth- and twentieth-century police files.

S.A. – This also reveals the aspect of American culture that mythologizes the outlaw, who has a very ambiguous role in our society. Outlaws are thought of as heroic, as part of that ideal of the American individualist.

C.A.M. – Do you see any parallels between *An Unusually Bad Lot* and your early project in Berlin, *The Writing on the Wall*?

S.A. – That is a very interesting question. It is a difficult comparison to make. The Berlin project was about genocide, which is so dramatic, with the abrupt removal of people from their homes and then their permanent disappearance.

C.A.M. – In the case of the Boston project it was a more insidious, less dramatic process that led to these people's misfortunes.

S.A. – Right, exactly. The two projects have more in common than they have differences if you get beyond the specific circumstances of these people's lives. In terms of contemporary media I try to do two things–to reanimate a site with images of its lost history, and to give voice to people who have, in one way or another, disappeared, either literally or in the way history is told.

C.A.M. – Perhaps you could talk about this in terms of your working process.

S.A. – I don't have a political agenda that I look to give visual form to. That is not the way I work. I try to create works of art that are complex and that provide the viewer with opportunities for reflection. Clearly the social and political are a key part of my sensibility, but it is also absolutely essential for me that the viewer has a visceral as well as an intellectual response to my work. The challenge for me is to create projects that engage the intellect, the senses and the emotions.

C.A.M. – It is clear that you begin with an emotional response to something…something that "hits you in the belly."

S.A. – I respond very strongly to spaces, places and architecture. As an artist I want to amplify the sound of buildings murmuring or whispering. It is as though I am taking a stethoscope, as if I were a doctor, and laying it onto a façade and listening. Of course that analogy can only go so far. My method is not in any sense objective. I have to feel fully consumed and engrossed. Otherwise it is easy enough to come up with a one-liner concept. You could have ten of those a day if you wanted to.

Shimon Attie, *An Unusually Bad Lot,*
2nd Annual ICA/Vita Brevis Project
projection texts

Her delinquent career began at a early age. She has very early recollections of immorality.
She is blue and moody. She thinks one of her parents was colored and one was white.
He was locked up for being a stubborn child who stubbornly refused to submit to the lawful and reasonable commands of his mother.
She showed no appreciation for their efforts to interest her in church work. They could not control her.
...lazy, listless, quarrelsome, inefficient, lacks persistence, stubborn, careless and inclined to be slovenly.
A sensuous and repulsive-looking man. He looks as if he might have easily committed any of the crimes of which he is charged.
She was arrested with a colored man and invariably gave some answers much colored.
Positively tricky, this woman talks without moving her lips. Her habits are tea and sex.
As a class, they make excellent servants and I doubt if any training would qualify him for any other line of work.
It is an ungracious and ugly thing to happen. She was probably as much to blame as he.
Her family objected to having her around on account of her skin disease.
Nothing is known of him. He was living off a prostitute, apparently a victim of his own ignorance.
I hope religion will win with our girl. We want to get hold of her by all the handles we can.
Her uncle states that she is the black sheep of a highly respectable family.
His memory is good regarding names, dates, and past events of his life. He will undoubtedly make a very good inmate.
She was rough and lawless and seemed a little queer mentally, an awful tomboy.
Her pastor thinks the only humane thing for the girl is institutional care, which is extended to persons of her class.
They committed the crime of adultery with each other by then and there having carnal knowledge of the body of the other.
She hates sewing and housework. She is a willful, headstrong, stubborn young woman.
He is suspected of performing illegal operations and engaging in perverted sex practices. He must be closely observed while incarcerated.
She did not seem to feel ashamed being arrested for fornication, not even with a colored man.
3 crooked fingers, good home, bad reputation, a slick young man and not to be trusted.
It cannot be taken as psychopathic sexuality as this sort of thing is very common among Greeks.
She is not so ugly, but is a rather stout, sloppy-looking woman with coarse features.
Just a naughty child. She could not stop going to theaters and moving pictures.
They then and there did feloniously and unlawfully commit an unnatural and lascivious act with each other.
She says she did it not from perversity but under the pressure of poverty. This is nothing but an expression of her low standard of values.
He is something of a verbalist and has a reputation as a homosexualist.
She always wanted to dress with a flash. She would cut off high-heeled shoes to make low ones.
Of mixed Indian and Negro parentage, he could not resist the natural temptation of such a cosmopolitan birthright, and he followed the dictates of his unstable mind.
Without having evidence of actual immorality or even indecency, we always knew all of her interests were common.
She is very explosive, loses her temper and is very unreasonable until made to toe the mark.
We should consider her defective mentally, very subnormal, probably a moron.
His love of sports should be reawakened with the intention of discouraging his sexual irregularities.
The morals of the family are the lowest. Even a moral girl would be contaminated by living there.
She says the needles won't help. She says she is already half wild.
There was every indication she was an unusually bad lot.

Art on the Emerald Necklace

The 3rd Annual ICA/Vita Brevis Project
Summer 2000

Conversation between James Boorstein and Carole Anne Meehan about *Emanations*, Art on the Emerald Necklace, 3rd Annual ICA/Vita Brevis Project

Carole Anne Meehan – *Emanations* was the result of an extraordinary investigative process, centered around the development of a circular-wave-making machine. This probably sent you down roads you didn't expect to travel. Is that true?

James Boorstein – For once in my life I thought I was going to try not to reinvent the wheel, which I have done too many times. I wanted to locate existing technology that would do what I wanted it to do, so the whole beginning of the project was a search for that. It slowly unfolded that I wasn't going to find the right existing technology and that I would have to figure it out myself. A lot of my work ends up being about the exploration of materials in this way.

C.A.M. – It seems that this aspect of your work satisfies the scientist or inventor in you.

J.B. – Yes, although the true materials here are water and waves. Not that a wave is really a material, but I was trying to figure out things like, what does a wave actually look like? What does a wave feel like? How do you work with it? How does it start? How does it end? All that kind of stuff.

C.A.M. – I suspect you take great joy in being outside for prolonged periods.

J.B. – I like to be outside. Living in New York City I don't get much opportunity to work outdoors. One can walk outside or sit outside, but then you are not usually engaged in a particular activity, apart from sports, which I don't play. There were a lot of tasks to do for *Emanations*, starting with getting all these gadgets and equipment properly placed at the pond. Being able to spend day after day outside, working on the piece, was a great pleasure.

C.A.M. – And you needed to use your diving skills.

J.B. – I don't know how I would have completed this project otherwise. Though I have diving experience I have never actually done work underwater. Apart from professional divers I don't think many people would do this. Something as simple as hammering was extraordinarily difficult underwater. With so much silt in the pond I could not see my hand in front of my face so leveling the devices and tightening all the parts in place was a significant challenge. It is a completely different world, even just a few feet under.

C.A.M. – Would you talk about your exploration of the Emerald Necklace prior to selecting a spot in which to work?

J.B. – I walked the entire Necklace from the Boston Common all the way to the far end of Franklin Park. Along the way I found several places that I wanted to work. One idea that I considered for the longest time was about sharing the experience of spending a night outdoors, with urban people in a nearby woodland, most likely the Arnold Arboretum. I let go of this project

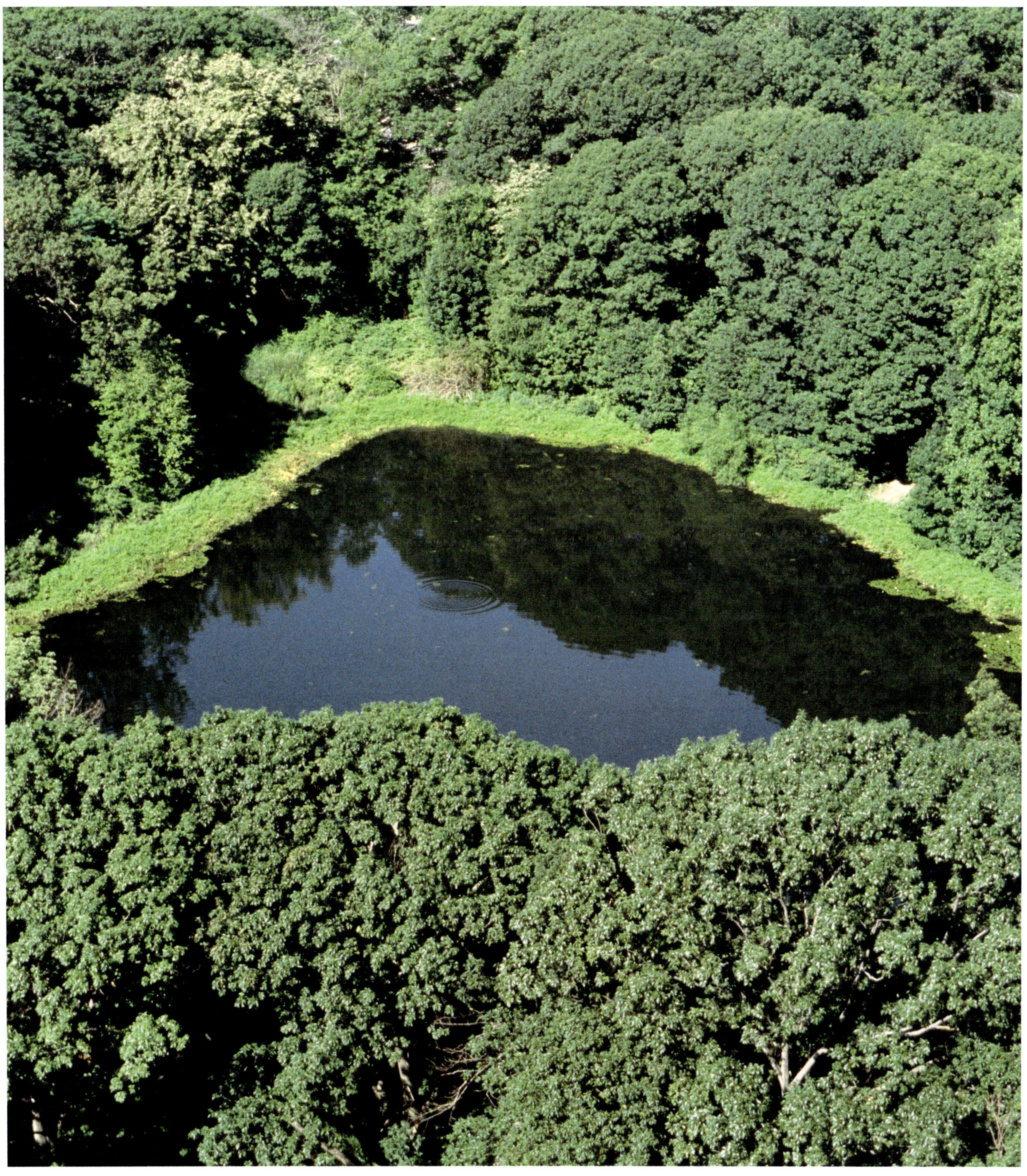

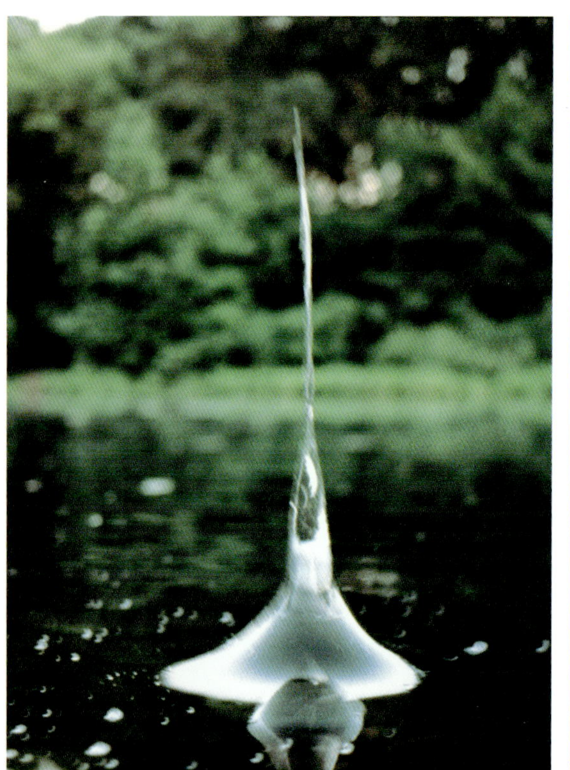

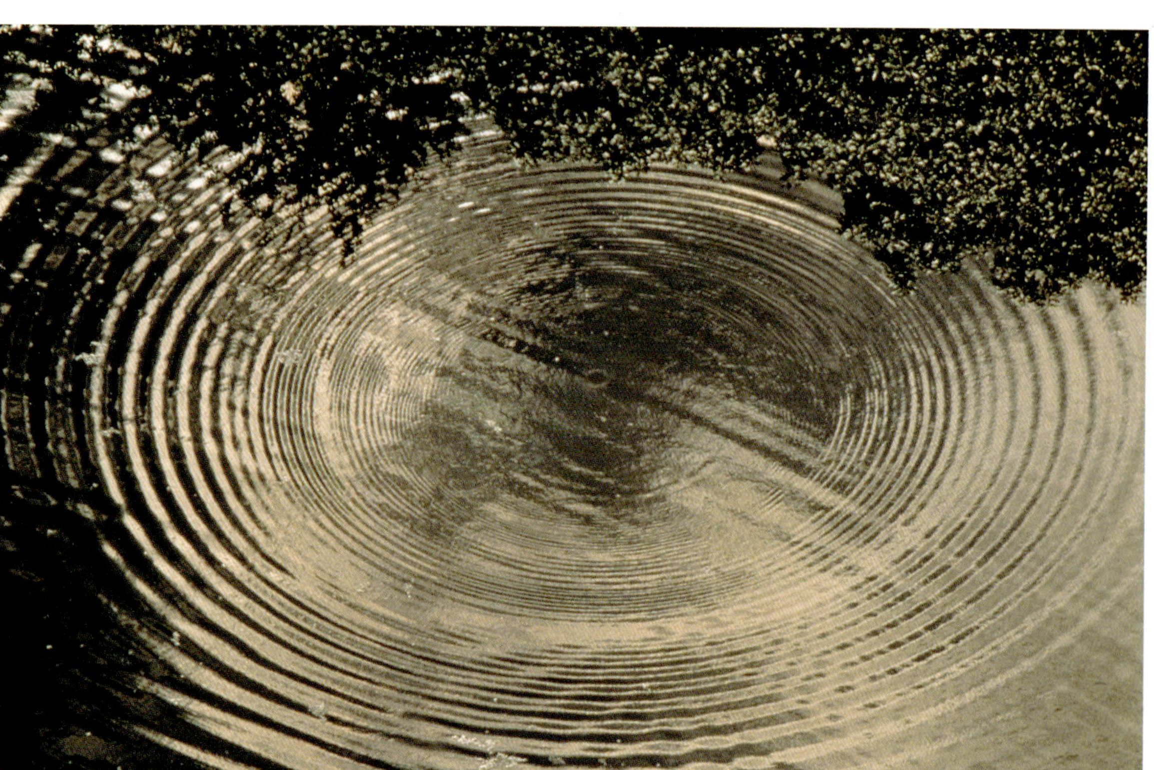

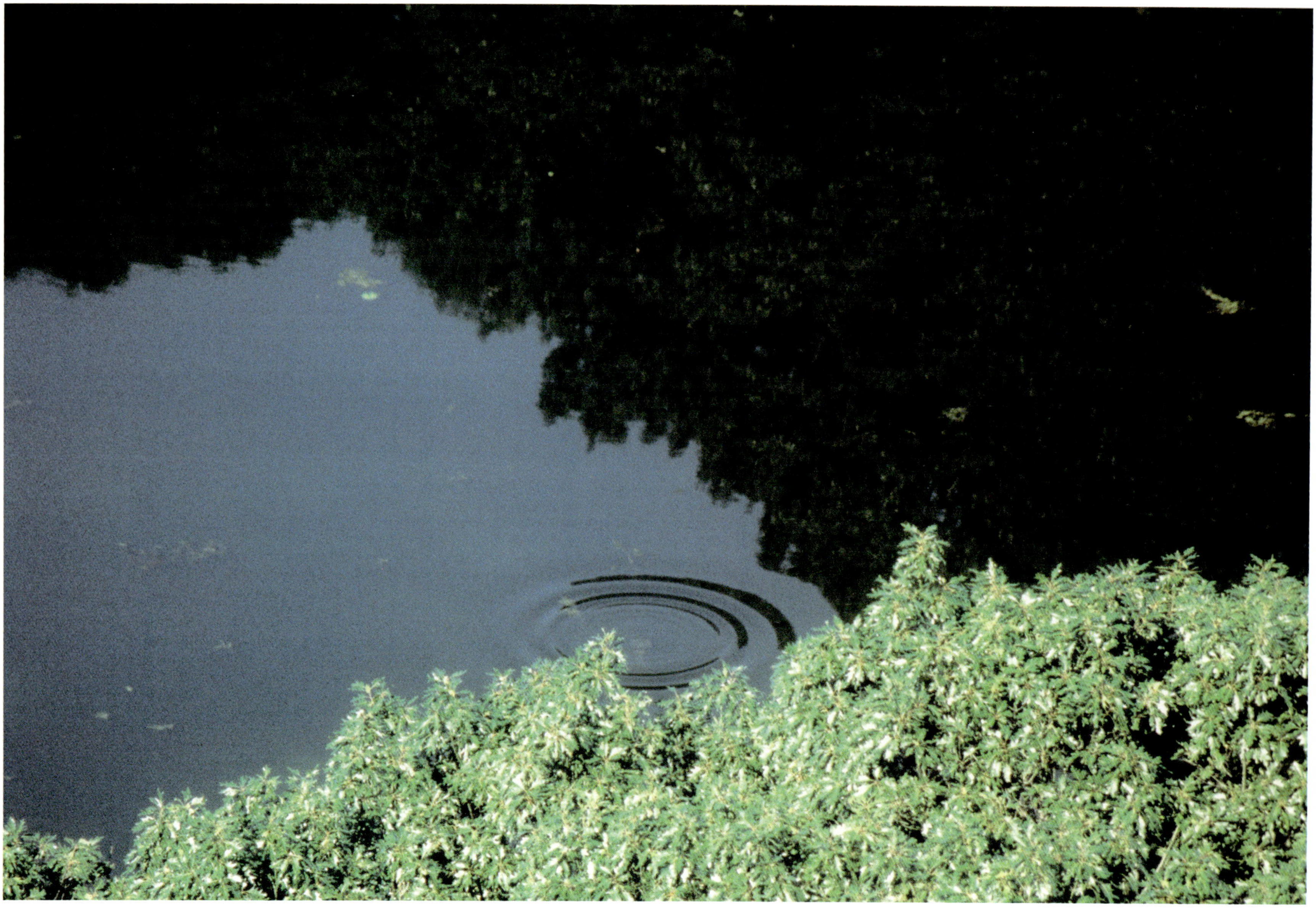

because I realized that I was going to end up as a camp counselor of sorts. The second time I walked the Necklace I was trying to be open to places that seemed powerful in some way, or special, and there were a few. Ward's Pond won out in the end because of the pure stillness I found there.

C.A.M. – What were some other things that drew you to Ward's Pond?

J.B. – The perfect reflective quality of the pond's surface; it really held my attention. The whole area is magically isolated from the city. Another thing I liked about the site is that you can walk all the way around it. I have been working on a project relating to walking around the island of Manhattan for twelve years, so this was an important connection that I only realized later. Being outside and looking is what my work is about. I am walking, but I am walking as a sculptor.

C.A.M. – I believe you said there were seven ideal vantage points along the pond's perimeter from which one could observe the piece.

J.B. – Yes. The thing that made me the happiest, in a way, was that some people came numerous times and just parked themselves in a particular spot. Most people chose a sandy hill which was, in the end, not really the best place to see *Emanations*. I do not have a scholarly knowledge of Olmsted's work, but I know that sight lines were important to him. The area has changed considerably since he designed it. Over time, it has become increasingly overgrown and closed in, making it more intimate in a way that I like. The natural growth now blocks the view in most places, but reveals it at others. So, in unplanned ways his sight lines, or view corridors, are present in a powerful way.

C.A.M. – Using the piece to create an engaging experience seemed to be very important to you. Do you have any stories to share in this regard?

J.B. – I knew my idea was starting to work, creating something that could almost be natural, when a fisherman started casting out towards the circular emanations created by early tests of the first wave machine. In terms of creating a visual experience, someone commented that I was manipulating a gigantic canvas by working the entire surface of the pond. I guess this is true and was definitely part of my intent with the piece.

C.A.M. – The tranquility of Ward's Pond is obvious, but when I led groups to the piece, I was also very much aware of the sense of suspense, of waiting for the wave machines to perform.

J.B. – This is an important area to address. When people come looking for a work of art, the normal human expectation is "Well, where is it? What is it?" Experiencing *Emanations* was a little bit like whale watching. You know you are on a boat, and you wonder, "Where is the damn whale?" I think many were probably disappointed in that there was a lot of waiting. But others who stumbled upon the piece without knowing about it beforehand were pleasantly surprised, and eventually realized what it was, and then got into the timing of it. I think the piece was a bit of a barometer of people's psyche.

C.A.M. – And a barometer of their attention spans maybe? Or their ability to slow down?

J.B. – Yes. The absolute longest interval between any of the machine's movements was just over two minutes and the average interval was just under thirty seconds. I know that it felt much longer for a lot of people. Some people don't know if they ever even saw the work, which has been true of a number of things I have made, even in gallery settings.

C.A.M. – Through your giving all this care to this little pond it almost seems you helped to energize the area. Do you think it is fair to say that? Although I don't know how anyone would sense this necessarily.

J.B. – Well, I like the idea of that. As I became more concerned with trying to create, or at least enhance, real experience, after a long history of making objects in my studio, working outside began to make more sense. There is, of course, energy and attention, but when there is no object to create, some of that may go into the landscape. I guess for me one definition of good art is something that can change your experience of a place.

C.A.M. – And your awareness of the place is heightened.

J.B. – Yes. The sights and sounds are tweaked in some way, or our awareness of them is.

Conversation between Ann Carlson and Carole Anne Meehan about *Any Day Now*, Art on the Emerald Necklace, 3rd Annual ICA/Vita Brevis Project

Carole Anne Meehan – How did you come upon the site pictured in the photograph you used to develop *Any Day Now?*
Ann Carlson – A long-time collaborator, who was in Boston at the time, did some research for me and found the photograph.

C.A.M. – So the photograph came first and then it was matched to its source location?

A.C. – Yes. *Any Day Now* is part of a series of projects called *Night Light* in which I restage historical images at or close to the places where they were photographed.

C.A.M. – What was your reaction when you first saw the site after matching it to the photograph?

A.C. – Finding the site of the photograph resulted in a nice narrowing of the very expansive Franklin Park. I fell in love with the contrast between the photo and the entropy of the present-day site. It was like coming upon a dolman, something very old, but not ancient. It was overgrown so much that it had a romantic quality to it, with enough of the old cage still there. There was just enough intact that it had an echo of another time. It was almost classic. And later it seems to have been a place where teenagers partied. It felt hidden from the mainstream eye, reinforcing that romantic quality I mentioned. I found much resonance between the photo and the way I found the place in 2000.

C.A.M. – Would you talk about the importance of the accurate re-creation of the dress and the personal items belonging to the people in the photo?

A.C. – It was important for diving deeper into the resonance of the site, both from the standpoint of the way it is now and the way it is in the photograph. I am very interested in the idea of all of time being in the present. By replicating the way it was in 1915 with complete, beautiful detailing, we put everything that much more accurately into the present moment. The whole picture just jumps out and becomes a big relief, helping to collapse time.

C.A.M. – The image was made by a postcard company so it was most likely a staged photo.

A.C. – After doing these projects, I feel like all photos are staged now. (Laughs)

C.A.M. – How did you arrive at having the costumed performers use movement as opposed to your use of complete stillness in other *Night Light* works?

A.C. – It was a way to deal with the remoteness of the site. If you recall, we were concerned about how anyone would be able to find the project. Having the performers move in slow motion also spoke to the time-based play within the piece. The group was clearly from another era. Doing that slow motion spread over two hours helped people know that we were up to

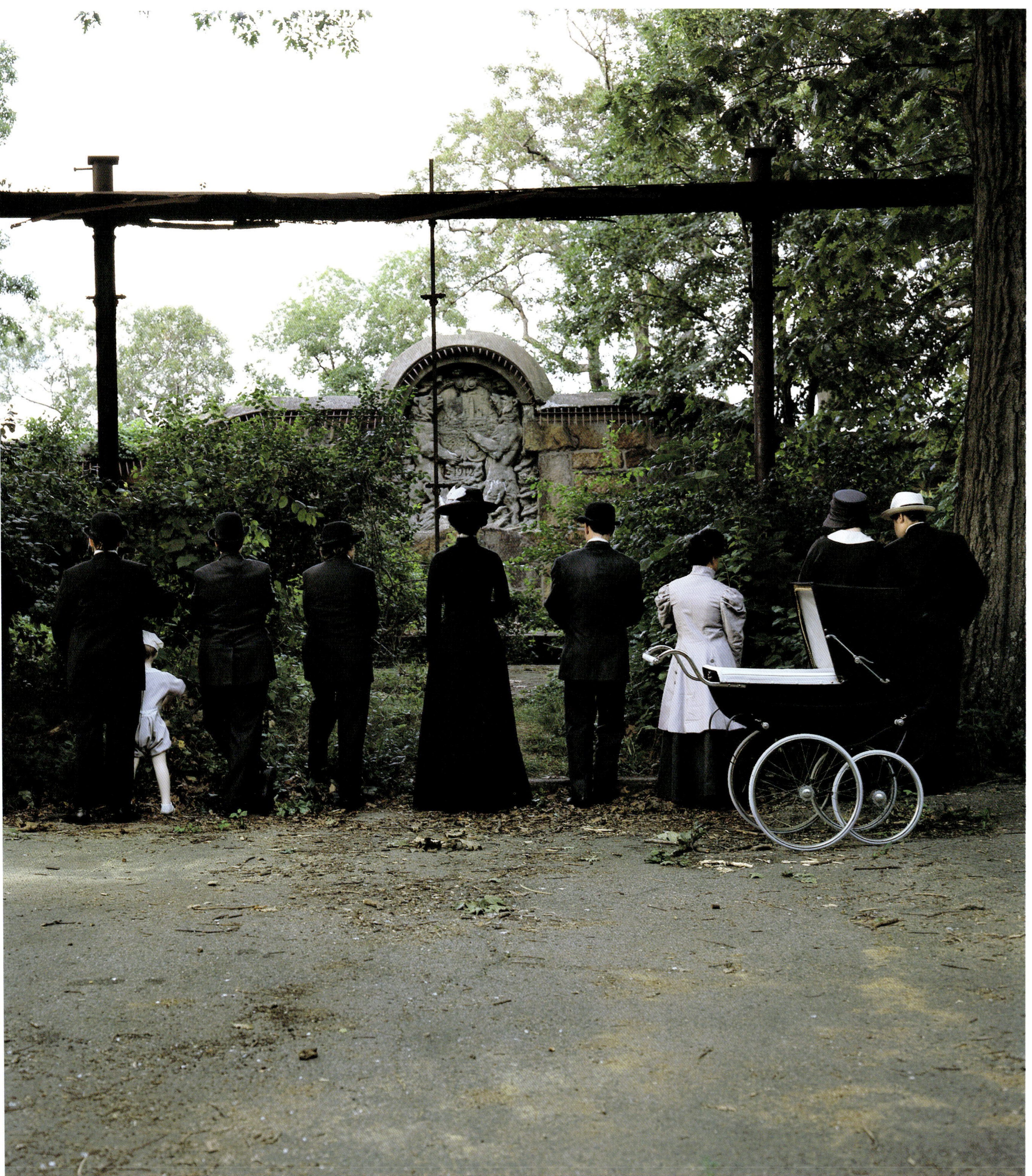

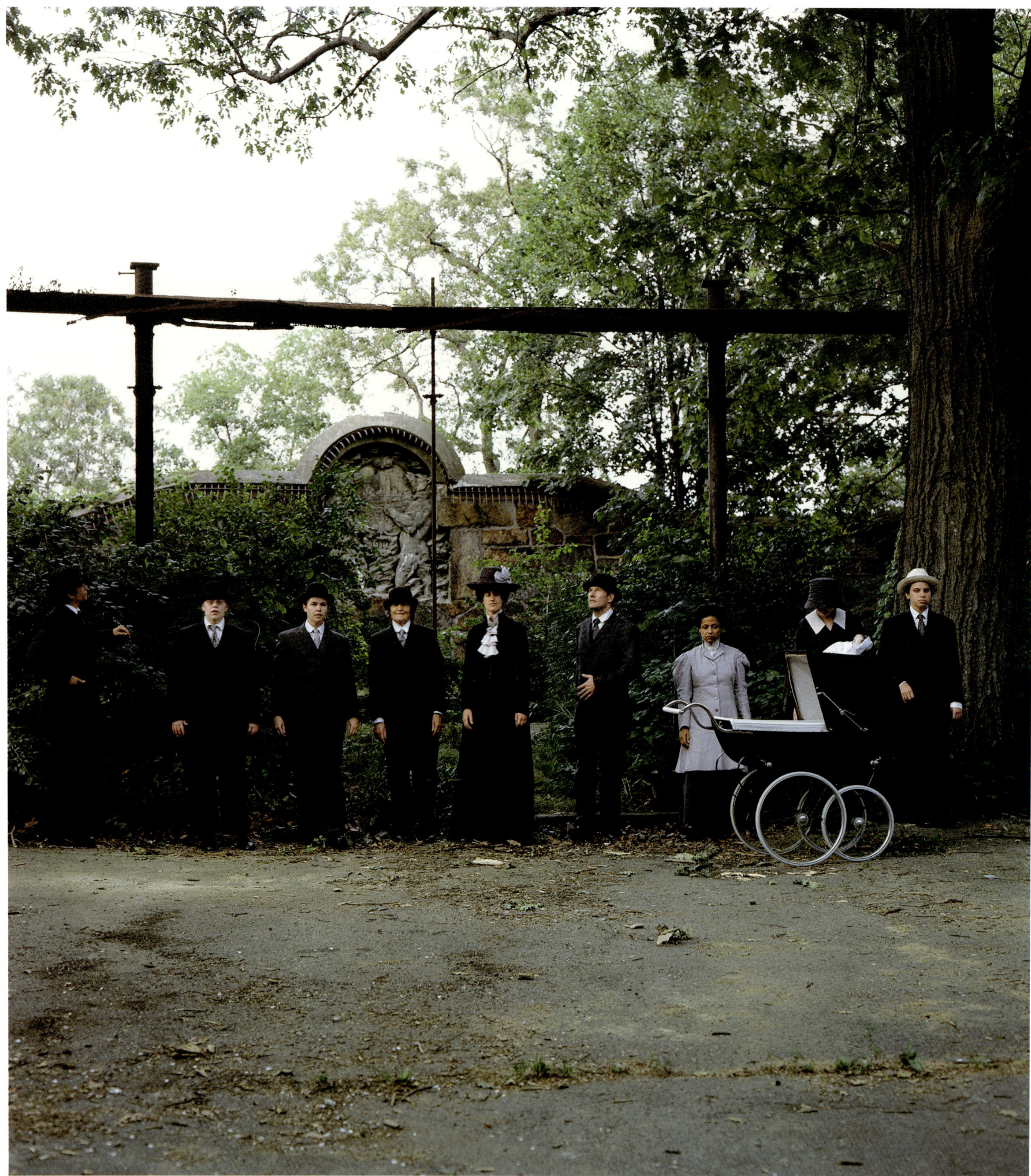

something. It helped to gather effect, gather spectators. And it accomplished that in a gentle way.

C.A.M. – A fascinating contrast was made when the contemporary park-goers mixed in and around the performers.

A.C. – That was good! Also, as I look back there were really wonderful and unsettling layers of meaning with our group passing through the park in the midst of a gospel festival.

C.A.M. – I thought about the day of the Boston Pops concert. That was really quite a moment that we chose strategically to be able to take advantage of a guaranteed audience. There were throngs and throngs of people. The gospel audience was more of a surprise.

A.C. – How did the Boston Pops come to be there?

C.A.M. – The Boston Pops is a venerable Boston institution, and this was the first and only time they performed a concert in Franklin Park. It was part of Boston's millennial celebrations in the summer of 2000. On the same day, Elma Lewis, a beloved community and arts leader, was honored. Lewis programmed another stage in the park during the 1960s and 1970s that attracted thousands of people to shows that had people like Duke Ellington. And we offered a slice of 1915. So three moments of the park's history were being highlighted – the turn of the millennium, a moment at almost mid-century, and then the early twentieth century.

A.C. – There were a lot of people there who were very excited about the presence of our colonials. (Laughs)

C.A.M. – Or early moderns. I was struck by how people seemed to understand that it was not simply an exercise in just displaying period costume. People's experience seemed to be more of the kind that raises the hair on your arm.

A.C. – Yes. I would say over and over to the performers that their job was to give life to an idea that these people from 1915 are still walking through that field. We just don't see them because of the way our consciousness is organized, but that on some level, they are actually still there.

C.A.M. – We did get that comment from one spectator about all the performers being Caucasian. It occurred to me that we had an assumption that the people in the photograph were Caucasian even though we were only seeing their backs.

A.C. – It becomes more problematic when we go back to the choice of the photo. Should I have asked myself if it will cause problems because everybody appears to be of European descent? Will it not be embraced within this neighborhood of so many people of color? It could have been an early short-sightedness in the selection. In choosing it I was thinking about place, not as a geographical spot in which people live, but just as a place that I am looking at.

C.A.M. – Yes, and the feeling of the place.

A.C. – And thinking about the effect of time on the place. Although I am reminded of Duchamp's quote that "every work has within it its expressed intentions and the unintentionally expressed." The way something from an earlier time is perceived now and within a different social context adds a whole layer to the work that was unexpected.

C.A.M. – The fact that we encountered this speaks to the strength of the piece, and its honesty, because it is just there.

A.C. – It was recreating that moment in time. We were going out on a limb a little bit to use slow motion, but ultimately the destination was a straightforward re-creation of an historical moment. You know someone used a photographic apparatus to set up the moment and we reset it up. This is a simple strategy but it gives rise to all this other, very complex stuff.

Conversation between Ellen Driscoll and Carole Anne Meehan about *Meanderlink*, Art on the Emerald Necklace, 3rd Annual ICA/Vita Brevis Project

Carole Anne Meehan – How were you affected by Olmsted's philosophy about public space? It seems you have a lot of appreciation for what he accomplished in his lifetime.

Ellen Driscoll – Yes, it is true. I did grow to love him. (Laughs.) Doing this project had a pretty big influence on me. My research led me to material that was more sustaining than I would have thought. I have applied some of his organizing principles to some of my projects that came after this one. In terms of the long life of his impact it is almost beyond reproach, I think.

C.A.M. – What were Olmsted's organizing principles that informed the creation of *Meanderlink*?

E.D. – In this situation I was mainly guided by his ideas about peripheral vision and an idea that he called "communicativeness." Olmsted made his walking paths in his parks meander in order to activate the stroller's peripheral vision. This occurs when turning back and forth on a winding path. This encourages the subconscious to become active.

C.A.M. – Did your embrace of this concept lead you to use the sky rather than the earth for the project?

E.D. – Yes. I thought I would use the sky and make everyone look up and out. That's how I came to the idea of flying a banner in the sky. Also, Olmsted's parks are so beautiful that if you put something in the park you might actually take away attention from the beauty of the park. I wanted to avoid doing that.

C.A.M. – What about "communicativeness"?

E.D. – This notion influenced my thinking about the magazine that accompanied the project, which became this sort of pictorial poem that included a quote from Olmsted about "communicativeness." This essentially was his expectation that even if people are very unlike each other in terms of class or country of origin, they would feel more connected to each other simply by sharing the space of a beautiful park. As you know, we distributed the magazine on the ground, and made it free and available to anyone who wanted a copy.

C.A.M. – Would you talk a little bit about the image made for the banner?

E.D. – Sure. It consists of two figures tossing a map back and forth. It looks as if they are playing a game together. The map shows the spiral of the walking paths in Bussey Hill, an area in the Arnold Arboretum. I included an image of a tree, to again refer to the Arboretum, so it looks as if the tree is part of the game they are playing.

C.A.M. – Have you thought about how to assess the impact of this work of art you made that was literally airborne?

E.D. – I think of it as a bouquet toss, a gesture that was very much about letting go. But I haven't sat around wondering,

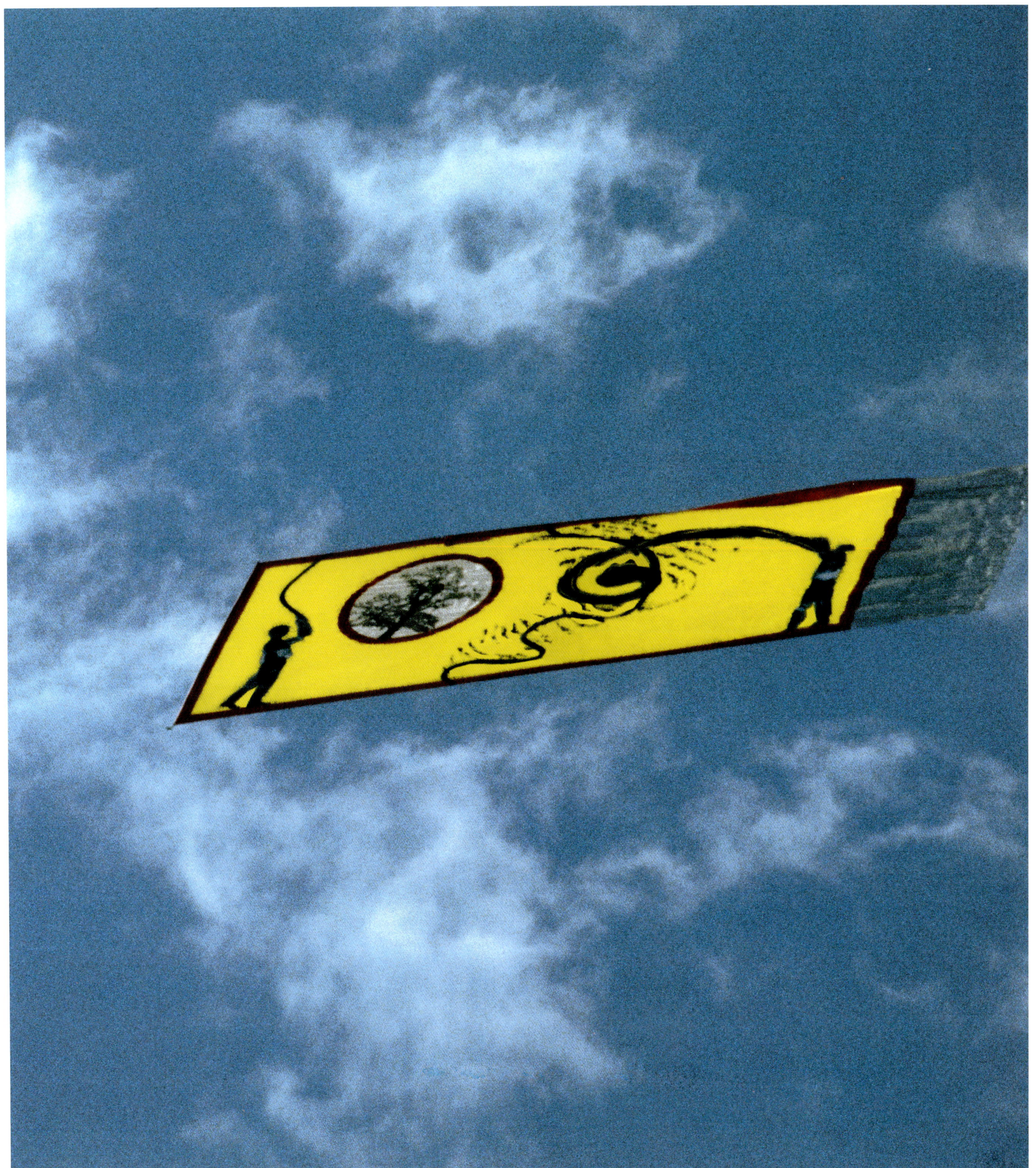

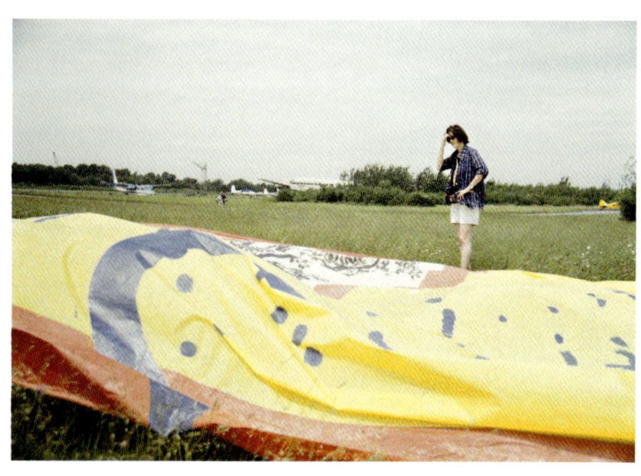

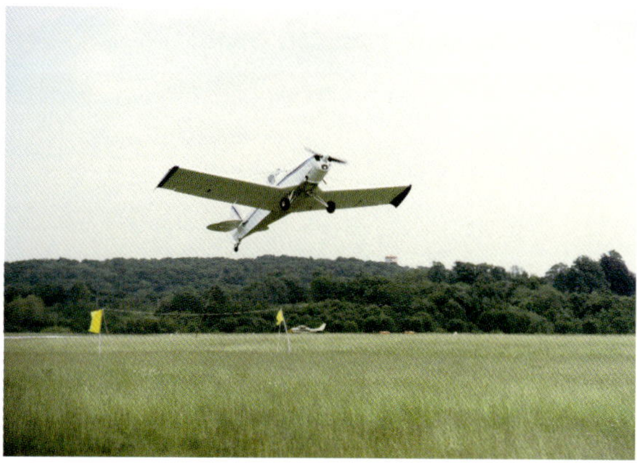

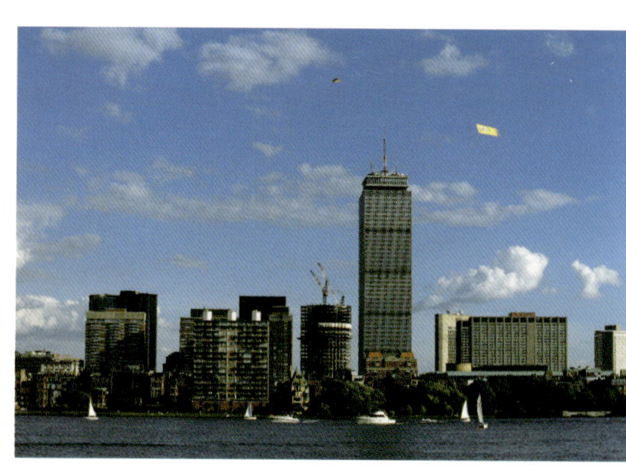

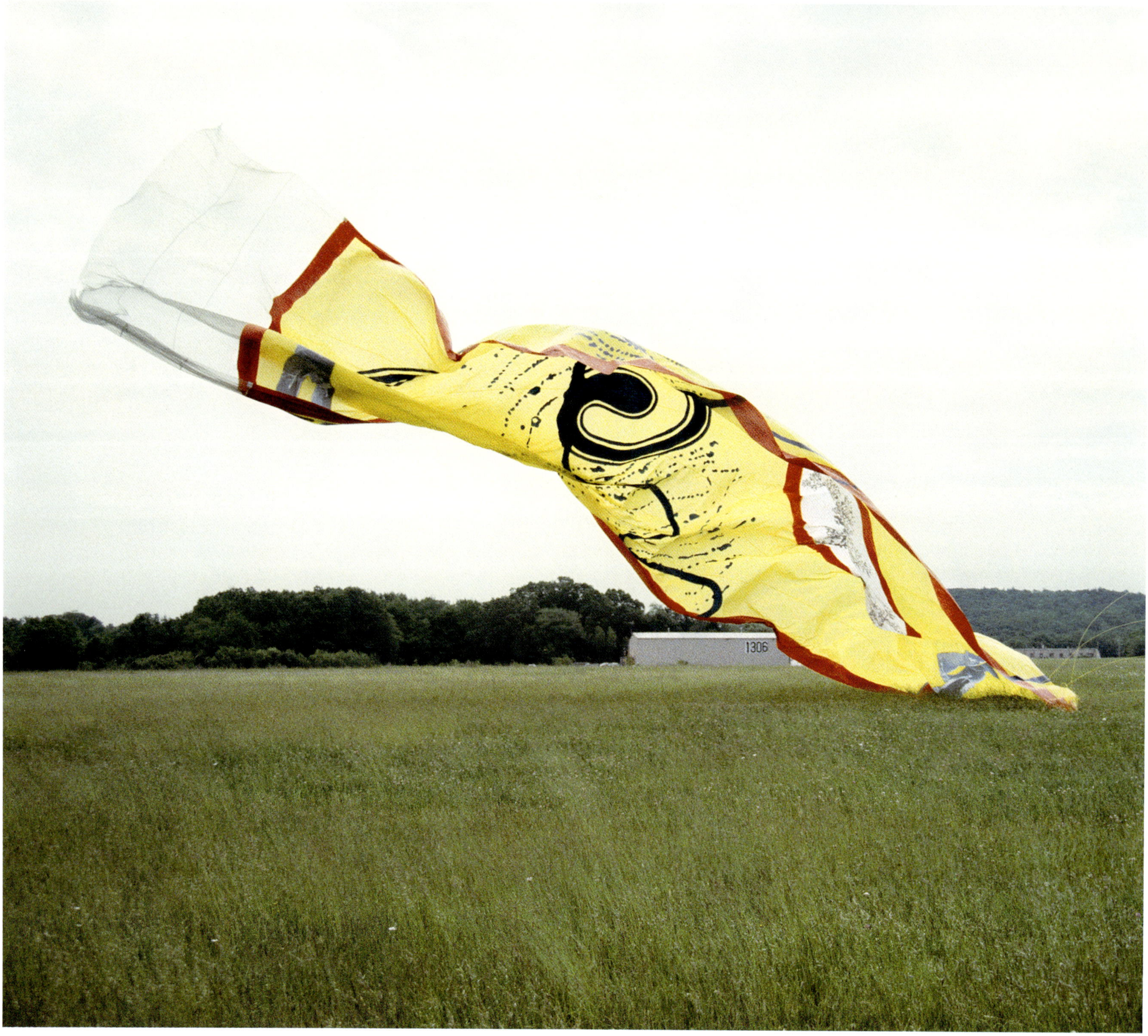

"Well, who appreciated it?" My friends would call me when they saw it in the air. But I will never know what the man on the street was thinking.

C.A.M. – What is your sense of the distribution of the magazine?

E.D. – The airplane flew over the path of the Emerald Necklace in its meandering way, but the magazine traveled on a different sort of circulatory system. I didn't get any specific feedback about the magazine, so I guess it was another kind of bouquet toss. It was something that I really enjoyed doing. I loved the Olmsted quote I used in it and I liked working in a "zine" format.

C.A.M. – Yes, it is a beautiful thing to have, the magazine.

E.D. – I don't know whether it worked to illuminate or clarify what I put up in the sky, or whether it was received as a completely separate thing. I actually have no idea. (Laughs.) Maybe I created it because I was concerned about people being able to understand the airplane banner. In the end, you don't know if it helped someone to connect the dots to the banner. Doing this project helped me to get comfortable with making such open-ended gestures.

C.A.M. – All of what you say is true, but what a gift to hear that hilarious story about some corporate executives who saw the banner outside of their windows as it flew past the downtown skyscraper that held their offices. They believed this spectacle was a desperate gesture by a company bidding on a contract they were about to award.

E.D. – One of the slightly subversive amusements here is that we were tweaking everybody's idea of what an airplane banner does. People don't expect to have pure visual pleasure given to them for nothing. You are supposed to have to pay for it or there is something to buy or there is some hidden message.

C.A.M. – Yes or what crazy institution would back it? (Laughs.)

E.D. – Right. Advertising is filled with sensuous pleasures because it is meant to make you feel desire of all kinds. When there is no product, people are mystified. Like, how could this not be an act of commerce? (Laughs.) Ironically, we had to buy the space so that we could use it for something other than a commercial purpose.

C.A.M. – It was an interesting assumption those corporate executives made about what they saw right outside their window.

E.D. – Their very first thought was that it was an advertising campaign of a competitor. Advertising these days doesn't always name the product, but sometimes uses visual teasing. They probably thought that this was the first in a series of teasing signs and signifiers to come. Also, I think this story tells you that people in tall buildings were seeing a lot more of the project, especially on the weekdays. In fact, it may have had more of an impact on people in these structures than on people walking through the parks of the Necklace.

C.A.M. – So does this story make you feel bad or good about one possible impact of the project?

E.D. – I think it is great because this is the kind of double-take that you want. People might get interested on that level and then they find out there is no act of commerce or corporate strategy represented by the image. It is a good thing for people to realize that these spaces in our culture can be used for another purpose. And many artists are doing this now because it is a nice way of inserting something into the bloodstream of commerce and seeing what happens. But certainly in Boston this approach has been underutilized.

C.A.M. – Our perspectives on so many things have changed since 9/11. I doubt an artist would even propose a project like this today. The juxtaposition of the plane and the Hancock and Prudential towers made for quite a piece of photographic documentation. Nevertheless, those spectators in the skyscraper were treated to quite a visual feast. It is great that you chose a brilliant yellow ground for the banner. Against the blue sky it was quite magical.

E.D. – Yes. One critic described it as a butterfly. I thought this was a really nice way to think of it. When it was far away it was just this yellow thing, but if you could view it more closely, such as through a window high up in the air, you would be able to see its detail.

The prospect of coming together, all classes largely represented, with a common purpose, not at all intellectual, competitive with none, disposing to jealousy and spiritual or intellectual pride toward none, each individual adding by his mere presence to the pleasure of all others, all helping to the greater happiness of each.

Frederick Law Olmsted on public parks, 1870

Conversation between Barnaby Evans and Carole Anne Meehan about *Moving Water*, Art on the Emerald Necklace, 3rd Annual ICA/Vita Brevis Project

Carole Anne Meehan – Would you talk about how *Moving Water* relates, or not, to your other projects?

Barnaby Evans – My work is usually very place based and is concerned with issues of space, ritual, symbolism, and phenomenological experience. The perceptual pleasures we receive from our empirical exploration of the world are often in the foreground. But *Moving Water* is actually a deliberate departure from much of my other work. It is more overtly political, historical, and conceptual, less concerned with pleasure or spectacle.

C.A.M. – Although the project uses water as its central element, which is a recurring practice in your work, especially in the well-known *WaterFire*.

B.E. – The centrality of water to our lives and to our world was my first interest in thinking about the Emerald Necklace. Olmsted threads water throughout the park system and uses its linear energy to animate the parks, guiding people through the newly created landscapes. The ICA commission seemed an opportunity for me to follow his cue and investigate water in its natural setting, rather than as a symbolic element, which is how I approach water in *WaterFire*. This led me to look at Olmsted's attention to the environmental context of water in his design. On exploring Olmsted's plan, the subtle complexity that he wove throughout his design became apparent and *Moving Water* became an opportunity to draw attention to the genius of his design.

C.A.M. – Would you elaborate upon how this context differs from the one you address with *WaterFire*?

B.E. – *Moving Water* is concerned with environmental politics and historical development rather than aesthetics. You could say it is industrial rather than beautiful, and theoretical rather than emotional. It does not engage the sublime or offer the spectacle of *WaterFire*. It is anonymous, which is a significant distinction from the recurring presentation of *WaterFire* that has many thousands coming to each presentation. *Moving Water* still deals with procession and spectacle, but in a more industrial way. Its spectacle, with the photogenic *ballet mechanique* of the bright red trucks and their highly polished reflective tanks, is more in line with the mechanical drama of a construction site.

C.A.M. – Would you talk about your early impressions of the Emerald Necklace that influenced your planning for this project?

B.E. – While exploring the Necklace I was flooded with impressions and ideas. One of these was to address the processional aspects of the waterways that form the park's connections. The Emerald Necklace alternates between corridors of passage and refuges of sanctuary. The arching trees pierced by the flowing water of the Muddy River, the pedestrian paths,

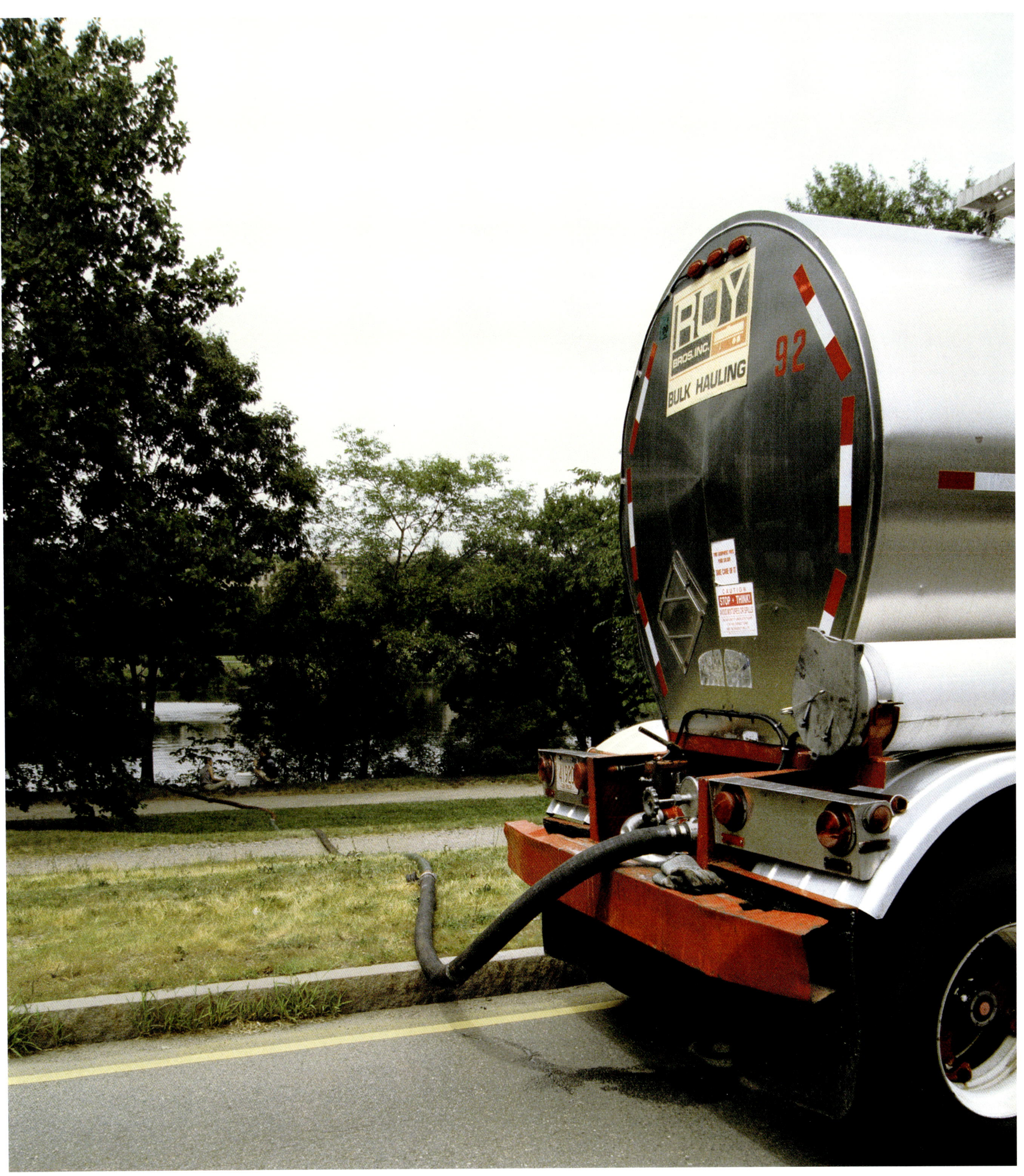
ROY
BROS.INC.
BULK HAULING
92
CAUTION
STOP • THINK!

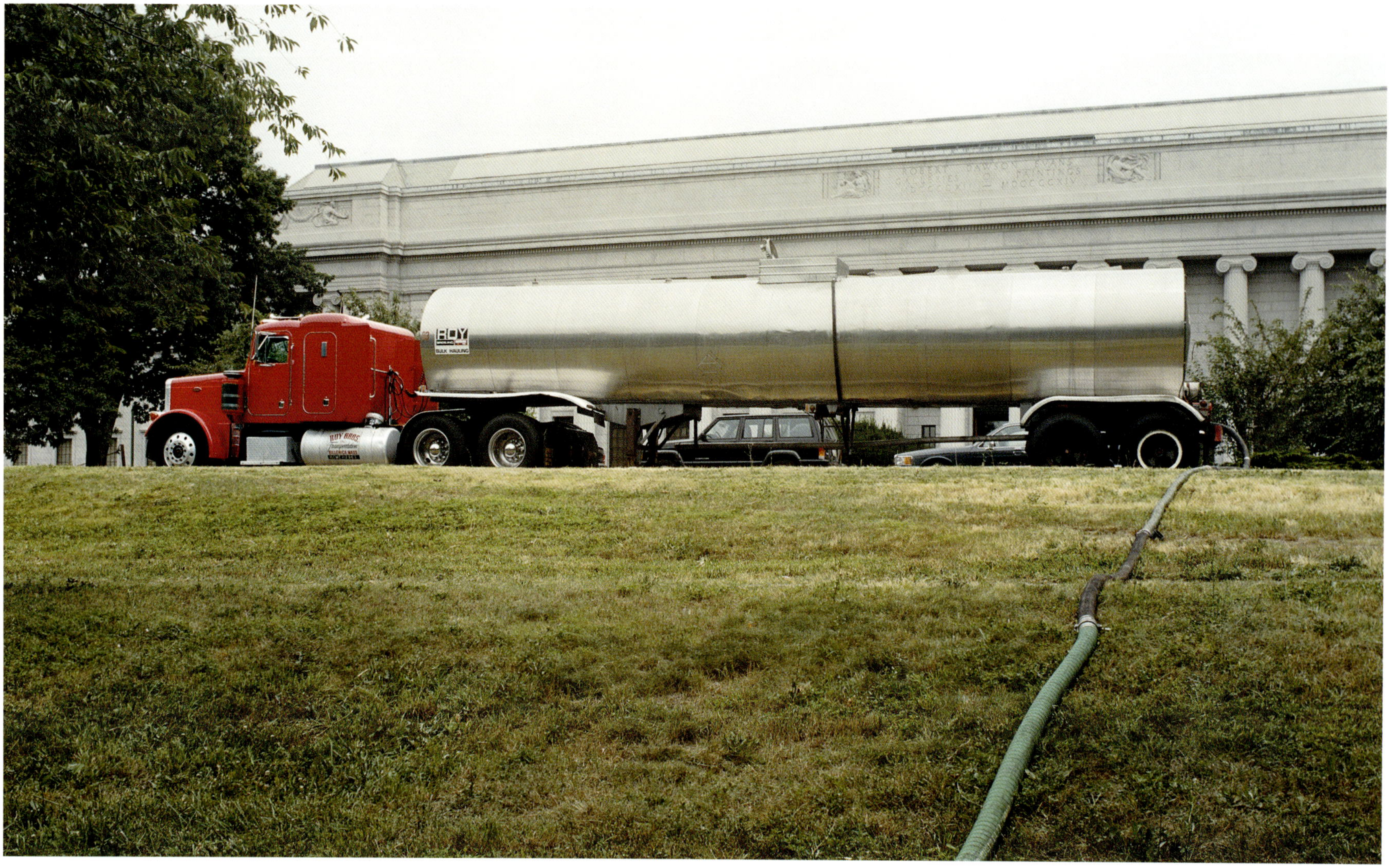

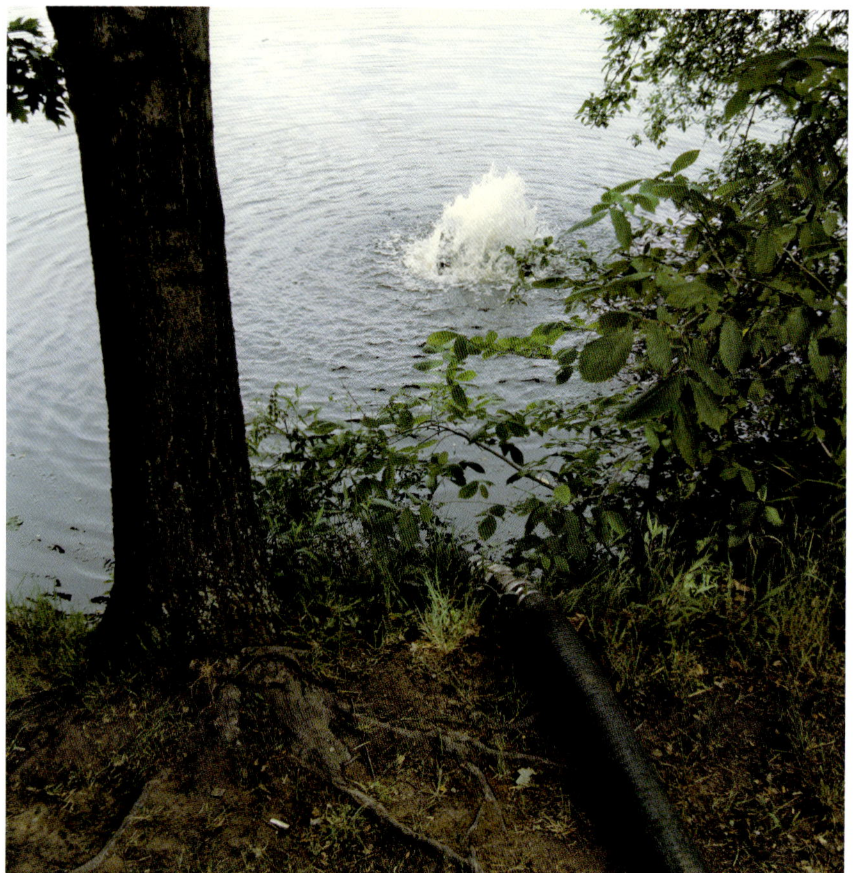

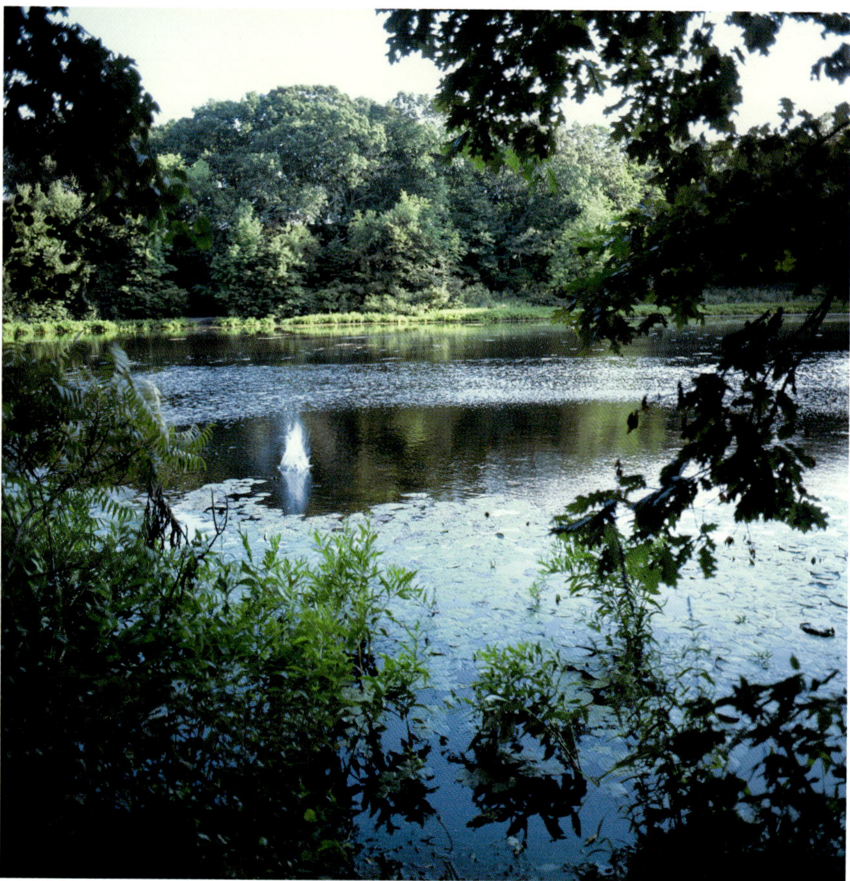

and even the parallel MBTA tracks all create a remarkably dynamic site with great energy, presence, and motion.

C.A.M. – So, in light of that, can you talk more specifically about how your ideas for *Moving Water* occurred to you?

B.E. – When I walked further down the Muddy River to the Back Bay Fens, the contrast between the slow, turgid flow of the lower river to the sparkling energy of the waterway upstream struck me. I began to wonder about the difficulty that Olmsted faced in creating an artificial landscape and thought of the hubris with which mankind presumes to tamper with large natural ecosystems. It was a great realization to learn that Olmsted had considered the subtleties of the ecology and hydrology with remarkable understanding and precision and had apparently created an artificial working stream that also solved the sewage backflow and flooding problems of the area. To learn that his elegant, environmentally correct, and technologically appropriate solution had been made ineffective as the result of the far less well conceived damming of the Charles River seemed to be an interesting object lesson. I wondered to what extent the subtlety of Olmsted's design, the success of its solution, and the very invisibility of its mechanical system had contributed to its eventual dismantlement. I hoped to address some of these issues in *Moving Water*.

C.A.M. – Which of these issues in particular were you hoping to highlight?

B.E. – What fascinated me about Olmsted's solution was its simplicity and its effective use of existing natural forces with only subtle interventions made to achieve his goals. Olmsted's design involved no pumps or electricity, no labor or human intervention, and very few moving parts, yet it solved the severe flooding problems of the Fens, eliminated the serious daily sewage backflow and gave the Muddy River sufficient flow and oxygen to achieve ecological vitality. Olmsted's use of the twice-daily tidal fluctuations to power the system is a brilliant use of alternative energy. The design was powered by the moon, and was capable of moving a massive amount of water without any human effort, day after day. The entire fleet of trucks engaged in *Moving Water*, working all day for three Saturdays gathering water from the Charles River and then releasing this same water into the Muddy River, could not even come close to moving as much water as Olmsted's original system did in a single morning's tidal cycle.

C.A.M. – The project certainly had an element of humor. There was an absurdity to your heroically performed, yet futile, repetitive actions to save and clean the river. This must relate to the frequent use of ritualized action in your work, although in this case it is very utilitarian with its own, crazy beauty.

B.E. – Charlie Chaplin's *Modern Times* comes to mind with its sped-up action sequences. But the intention here was to call attention to the effort and energy needed for man to do what had been accomplished without effort, twice daily, by the gravitational pull of the moon. This emphasized the near-comic incommensurability of our efforts and the immensity of the natural systems that surround us.

C.A.M. – What about the invisible, anonymous aspect of the project? The trucks were very visible, big disruptions to the landscape, but also invisible, not attracting the curiosity of passersby.

B.E. – Central to my intention in *Moving Water* is the inversion achieved between the absolute invisibility of the completed artwork and the muscular, industrial, and visible intrusion involved in its creation. This invisibility seemed appropriate in that I was addressing absence in the Emerald Necklace. There are two absences that haunt this place: the blind dismantling of the intricate and ecologically necessary aqueous understructure that created the Muddy River, which was once hidden beneath the park; and the invisible artificiality of Olmsted's entire landscape program, which was the product of a heavy industrial construction project that brought forth a wooded landscape from the sea and marsh. Now that the parks are grown and occupied, with the sea and the dredges and tractors and trucks long gone, the impact of Olmsted's intervention and the man-made artificiality of his pastoral landscape has become invisible and the park is transformed into an authorless "work of Nature."

C.A.M. – And the traces of your work are also invisible, although we know that it left the Muddy slightly cleaner after the three days of moving the water from one spot to the other.

B.E. – Yes, that is true. But my aim was to create a nearly pure work of conceptual art. I wanted it to be so resolutely absent, so entirely invisible, that only the conceptual trace would remain. Water is a colorless, transparent, formless, and fluid element that is perfectly miscible and always moving. It is almost impossible to create a work of art out of water, a substance with no structure. The act of combining two bodies of water is both invisible and utterly unrecoverable as an object. All that can remain is the conceptual intention and the fleeting memory of those who witnessed it.

Conversation between Sheila Kennedy, Frano Violich, and Carole Anne Meehan about *Common Pleasures: Parkway*, Art on the Emerald Necklace, 3rd Annual ICA/Vita Brevis Project

Carole Anne Meehan – Would you talk some about your initial attraction to the site?

Sheila Kennedy – When we thought about the Emerald Necklace we imagined its large civic gestures and structures such as parks, rivers, and parkways. These reinforce the idea of nature in the city. The Msgr. William Casey Overpass is a single entity, a bridge, that links the Necklace's two largest parks, the Arnold Arboretum and Franklin Park, yet it is essentially a large piece of highway infrastructure. The unlikely juxtaposition attracted us.

C.A.M. – What were some of the ways that you wanted to use the overpass?

Frano Violich – Well, for one, we knew we wanted to bring a vegetable garden to it. This way a connection could be made between Olmsted's early career as a botanist and his writings about the "common pleasures" that parks and gardens offer those of us who live in the city and are therefore deprived of the natural landscape.

C.A.M. – You devised a very practical, ingenious plan for managing this vegetable garden.

F.V. – Yes. We studied which plants would grow the fastest since we had just eight weeks for the show, and worked with a nursery to develop a plant list that could survive the harsh "freeway" environment. We also arranged for the Boston Parks and Recreation Department to deliver water for the 50-gallon drums that we included in the installation.

C.A.M. – And these drums of water were your solution to the need to water the garden daily?

F.V. – Yes again. We contacted summer youth programs that provided volunteers to water the garden. Having some community participation in the project was very important to us. We also wanted the piece to make use of alternative energy and recycled materials. We found manufacturers who could help us locate the materials we wanted.

C.A.M. – Your strategy for bringing illumination to the overpass was very resourceful.

S.K. – We carefully studied the movement of cars across the overpass at night and day and selected materials such as the reflective tape "Reflexite" and photovoltaic film. These materials would create effects such as glimmers and glowing.

C.A.M. – Your recounting all of the above reminds me how efficient your approach to the overall project was.

F.V. – Our hope was to use materials that could be recycled or reused. In fact, we recently discovered *Common Pleasures*' fencing in our neighborhood at a construction site, with the "Reflexite" and photovoltaic film still attached! We borrowed 55-gallon drums, and purchased the fencing units, but we were able to return these to the contractor who, evidently, still uses them. We planned to compost the plants and soil, and to harvest the vegetables.

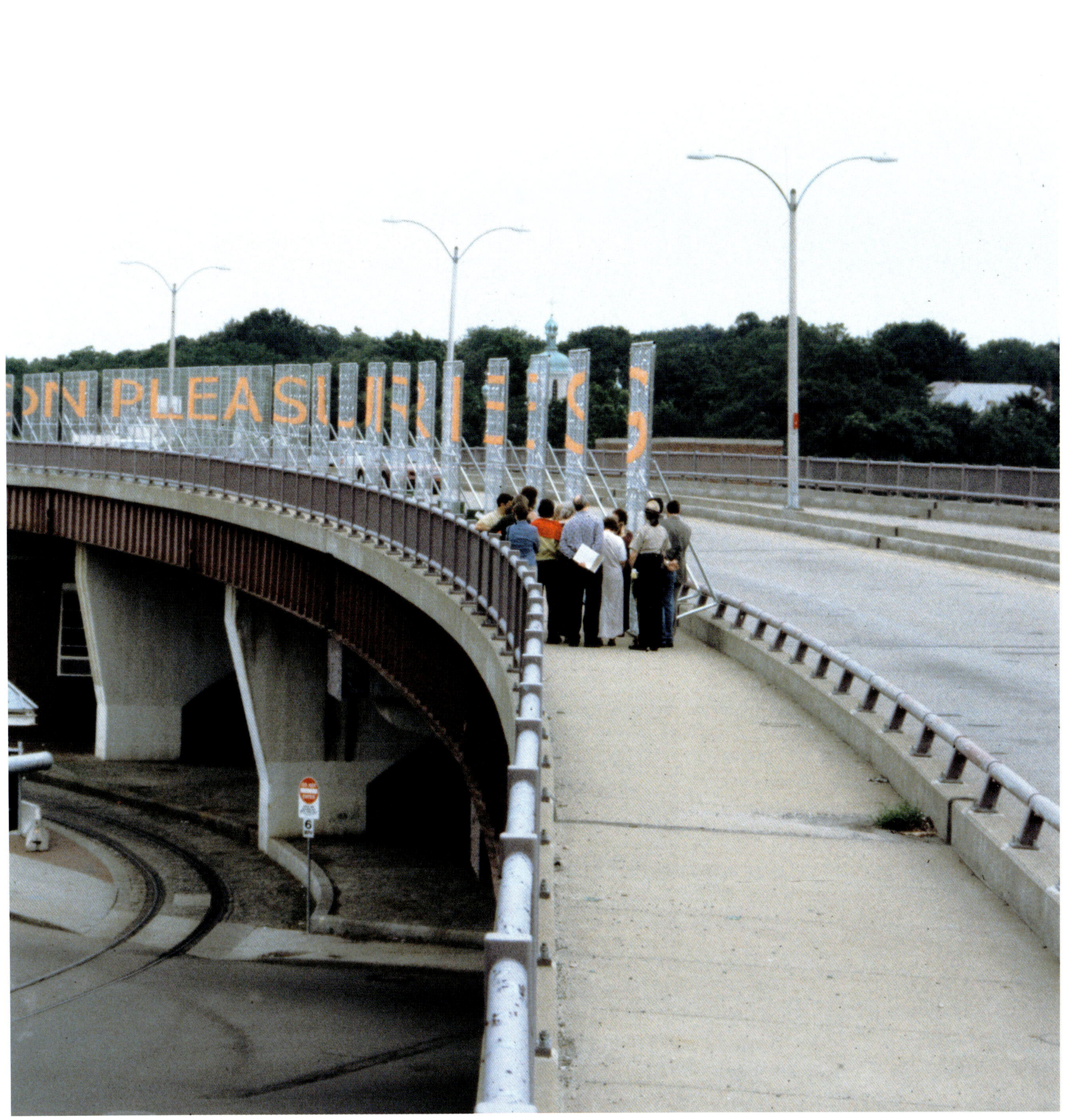

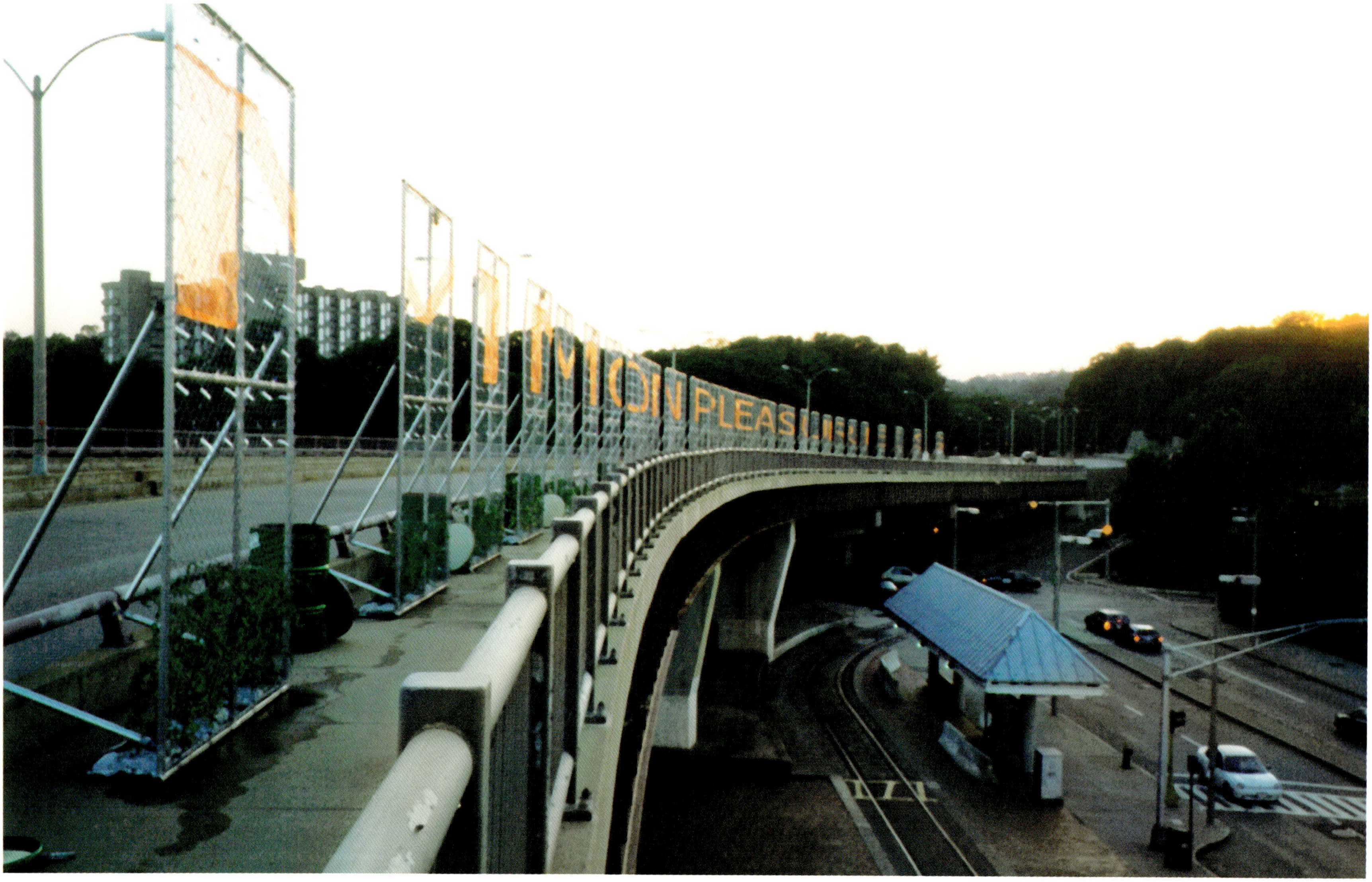

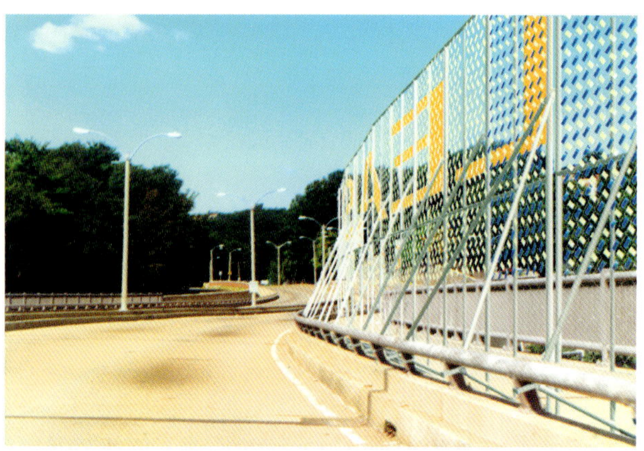

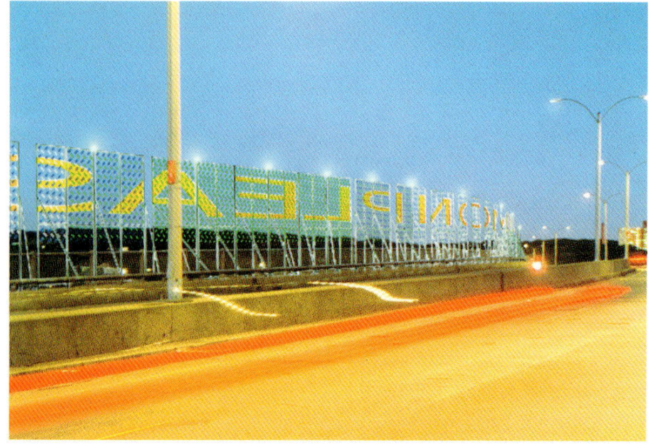

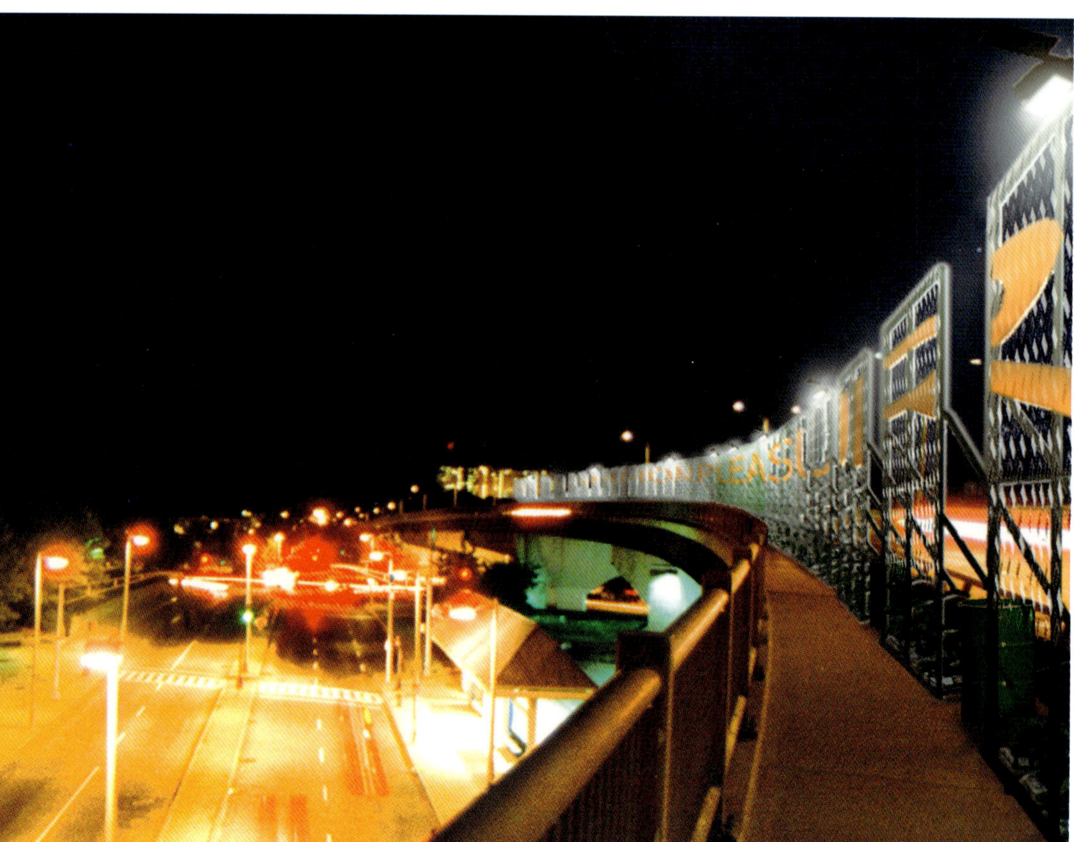

C.A.M. - Would you say the strategies you used for *Common Pleasures* tie into the overarching aims of your architectural practice?

S.K. – In many ways, yes. We are interested in relating the practice of architecture to contemporary culture and use materials as a vehicle to do this. We research materials and their properties and find ways to transform them using technologies such as solid-state lighting, digital design, and manufacturing.

C.A.M. – *Common Pleasures* certainly had a type of beauty and utilitarian elegance as a result of your use of some of these materials.

S.K. – We often use standard highway materials that can be cut up and stretched in ways that almost cloak their typical use. In this case we wanted them to help express our ideas about the nature of the parkway. The visual effects of reflectivity, glints, transparency, distortion, luminescence, and so on, are things we find in nature and that we regard as beautiful.

C.A.M. – You designed the work so that it could be seen from the perspective of both the pedestrian and those passing by in cars. This was quite a feat.

S.K. – We were challenged by the scale of the overpass, which is 7/10 of a mile long. It was designed for cars and not pedestrians, which is contrary to the goals of the Emerald Necklace. Yet the overpass plays a critical role in the success of Olmsted's intention to create a link between two of the Necklace's parks.

C.A.M. – Finding a way to entice pedestrians onto the overpass was one of your central challenges.

S.K. – We were very interested in luring the pedestrian onto the overpass. The sidewalks, which were not originally part of the 1950s design, were added in the 1960s when engineers realized the bridge was not structurally sound. The sidewalks on both sides became beams spanning from column to column.

C.A.M. – So the sidewalks were added to correct a major design flaw?

F.V. – Yes, but even so, the sidewalks were not really accessible. We were interested in creating a destination to attract the pedestrian public and reintroduce them to this important link in the necklace. To do this we made all of the project's elements over-sized so they could be easily seen from Forest Hills station, Main Street, and from a car passing by at 50 miles per hour. Once on the bridge, the smaller scale elements, like the plants in the garden, became a part of a separate, but parallel, experience.

C.A.M. – Is the urban, corridor garden of *Common Pleasures* somehow a comment on the scarcity of space in the early twenty-first century?

S.K. – No, because Boston is, thanks to Olmsted, a city with a wealth of parks and open space. It's more a comment on the over abundance of cars and how they, more than anything else, dictate the decision-making processes for urban design. We addressed similar themes in our Interim Bridges Project/Temporary City back in 1993.

C.A.M. – Your garden could also be seen as a humorous reworking of usual notions of urban community gardens.

F.V. – The utilitarian overpass contrasts so dramatically with the beauty of Franklin Park and the Arboretum. We were interested in creating an unlikely juxtaposition of a natural setting within a monumentally scaled artificial one. It is an extreme version of the victory gardens in the Fens or any garden for that matter. Extreme in every sense, such as the temperatures being so high on the overpass's concrete structure on those summer days that were over 90° F. Because of this the plants had to be watered twice a day.

C.A.M. – The garden is also a very pragmatic, remedial approach to the placing of natural materials in a stretch of roadway where Olmsted desired them to be.

F.V. – Just completing the project depended upon so many things. It needed so many special permits. It also required a collaborative effort from volunteers who helped build it and especially the neighborhood residents who watered the plants. The pragmatism of the project is reflected in the way that it was constructed and how it was maintained. Even the recycling of the light from passing cars that was absorbed by the photovoltaic strips has the feel of pragmatism to it.

C.A.M. – I am struck by the improvised, contemporary look of *Common Pleasures*. It is as though the work were declaring, "Olmsted had a great idea to put trees and greenery here, but in the twenty-first century we can't do it the way he would have."

F.V. – Yes, so we had to make the best out of a bad situation. Our intention was to bring the public to the site to experience it for themselves, and if they didn't do this, at least they may experience it from a passing vehicle in a different way. The hope was that the work would challenge their assumptions about public space along a highway.

C.A.M. – Perhaps we could talk some about how you see your treatment of this location as a potential model for the activation of under-utilized areas of the urban environment elsewhere?

S.K. – So many elements of the urban infrastructure, made during the 1950s era of "urban revitalization," such as bridges, elevated highways, abandoned rivers, waterfronts, canals, and so on, are great opportunities for artists, architects, and landscape architects. As our country's infrastructure begins to decay, there is an increasing imperative to create new public spaces and revive the areas and the communities around them. This has been one of the strengths of Vita Brevis, which has been a vehicle to open a debate about the use and fate of important sites, such as the Emerald Necklace.

Conversation between Cornelia Parker and Carole Anne Meehan about *At the Bottom of This Lake*, Art on the Emerald Necklace, 3rd Annual ICA/Vita Brevis Project

Carole Anne Meehan – Your work for *Art on the Emerald Necklace* is a part of your series involving the landing of meteorites. When did you begin this series?

Cornelia Parker – It started in 1996 when I inserted the iron from a ground-up meteorite into the fireworks of a pyrotechnic display in Tivoli Gardens in Copenhagen. The iron showed up as falling light, echoing, in a sense, its earlier fall to earth. The audience knew of the meteorite falling again through a series of signs in the gardens.

C.A.M. – How did it occur to you that the Emerald Necklace might be a good spot for one of your meteorite landings?

C.P. – I haven't made very many outdoor pieces. These tend to make me think of "the bigger picture." During my exploration of the Emerald Necklace I thought a lot about the relationship between the sky and the land. For this project I thought about actually putting the moon within the lake, or Leverett Pond, through the landing of a lunar meteorite. I wanted people to think about how the moon and the sky are reflected in the lake.

C.A.M. – It seemed like it was a very physical, factual thing that you wanted to accomplish. You wanted to complete, in a sense, the relationship between the sky and the water. We know that the moon is always above the water. But now, after your landing, it is below the water, too.

C.P. – As an extension of the idea, I put a star fragment into another lake. These acts are about trying to put something minute into a lake that ends up affecting the whole body of water, giving it significance as a repository of an astral body.

C.A.M. – What do you know about the history of the two meteor fragments that you used?

C.P. – The moon rock is from the Dag 700 lunar meteorite that was discovered in 1998 in the Libyan desert, although I believe the information about when it landed there is not known. The star fragment comes from the Allende meteorite, so named because it landed at 1:05 am on February 8, 1969, in a Mexican town called Pueblito de Allende. It contains particles that were formed during the explosion of a supernova that occurred before the formation of our solar system.

C.A.M. – Would you talk some about what you were hoping to accomplish with these two landings in the Necklace?

C.P. – I was thinking about how to create a piece of mythology for a public space. For this location, which is a series of connected parks used by a lot of people, I was aware that the audience for this work would be a cross-section of the general public. You have to have something that would be interesting and compelling to everyone, something that would capture their imaginations and their attention. For marking the occasion of these landings I thought I would use authoritative-looking

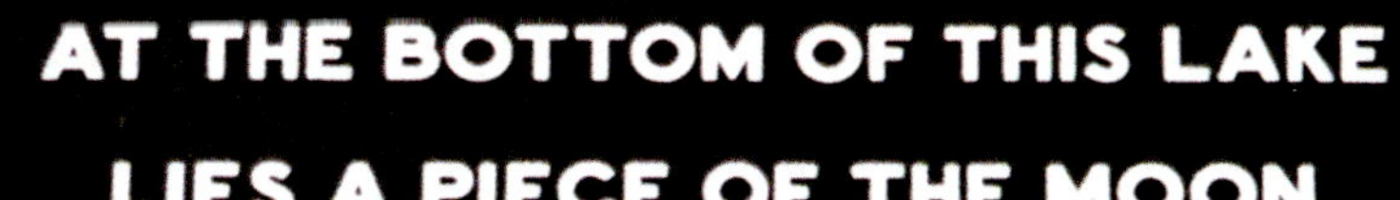
AT THE BOTTOM OF THIS LAKE
LIES A PIECE OF THE MOON
AT MIDNIGHT
ON THE 27th OF JUNE
IN THE YEAR 2000
A LUNAR METEORITE
FELL INTO THE BACK BAY FENS LAGOON

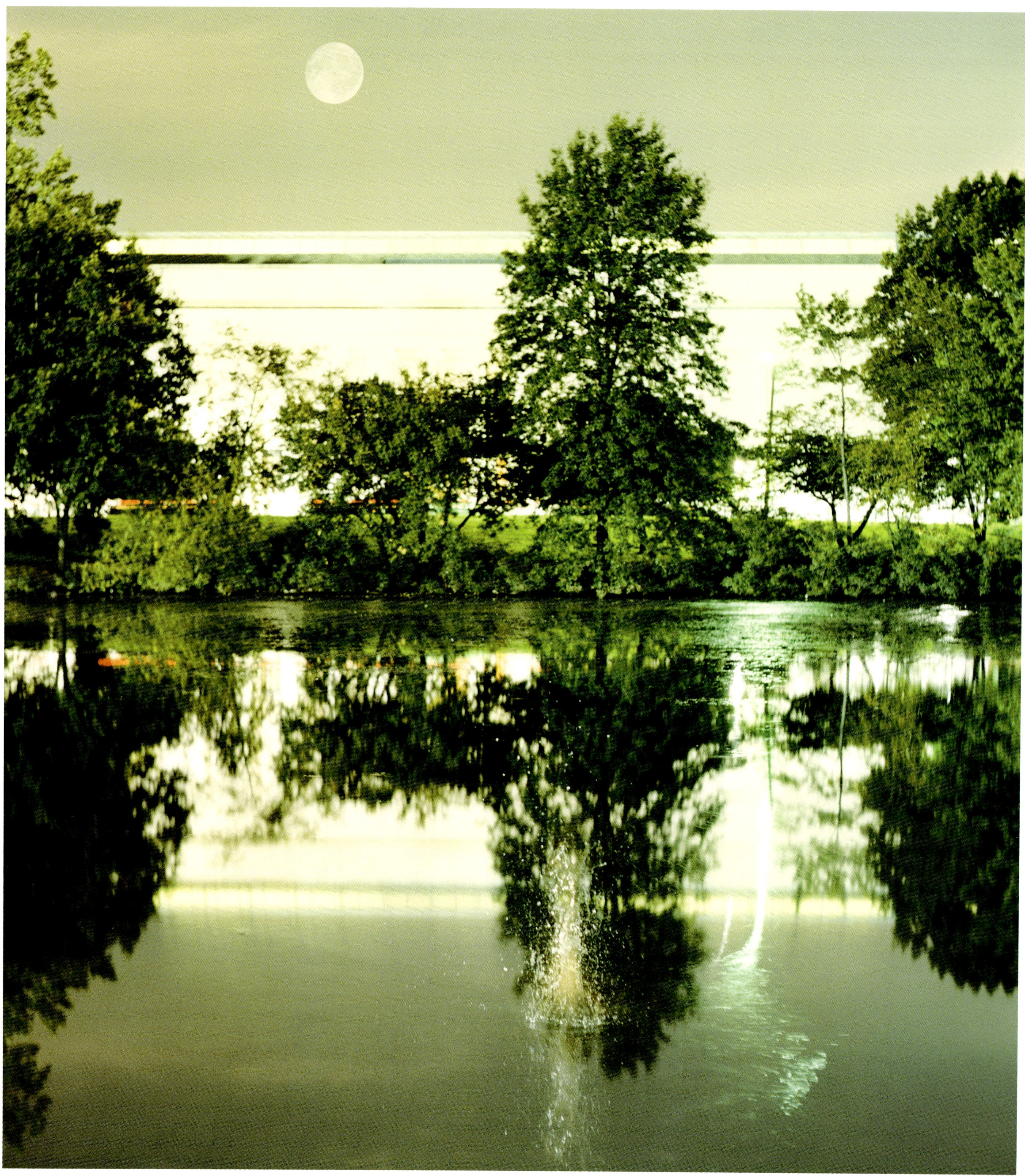

plaques. This would let people know, would officially declare, that the moon is now in the lake, for example. I wanted it to look as though the king had declared this to be true.

C.A.M. – And it is true. I know because I was one of the lucky witnesses to both of these landings. I recall you wanted these to be private events, and observed by just the people who had to be there. In addition to us there was a park ranger and a photographer. Also, you wanted to do this in the middle of the night–at midnight and at 1:15 am. This late hour caused the need for the ranger, for security. Was this the first time you have handled a meteorite landing this way?

C.P. – I developed a plan for the landings that would be specific for the creation of *At the Bottom of This Lake*. The occurrence of the landings at midnight and in very early morning was part of the mythology that I wanted to be an integral part of the work. Natural meteorite landings happen everywhere and are unpredictable. What I do is orchestrate meteorite landings in a variety of ways. Often these are public. If not, people can find evidence of the landing. The results, or the traces of these acts, or the naming of these acts by me, are hopefully what people can play with in their imaginations.

C.A.M. – Getting back to the signage, your strategy for the plaques was interesting. The text at the top was a poetic, open-ended description of the event. Below this, one could read the specific facts about the event, such as exactly what type of meteorite it was, the exact hour, and so on.

C.P. – The way I use text in my work is critical. It plays a very important part in the mythologizing of an object or a location.

C.A.M. – What responses did you imagine people might have as they encountered the plaques hovering above the water line?

C.P. – I hoped that whoever would see them would appreciate how this small, engineered event was monumentalized. And perhaps see the irony of this occurring only during the eight weeks of the exhibition. I have seen this kind of signage on government buildings and other official locations. It is full of authority and looks like it is going to be there for a very long time. What I really liked was that we placed our plaques in the lakes the very next day after the landing.

C.A.M. – Yes. Those who might have seen the work on the first day it was on public view would ask, how did these signs get here so quickly? The meteorite landed only yesterday! When we were looking for the best locations to place the signs in Leverett Pond and the Back Bay Fens Lagoon we had the signs out in public, if you will, before the landings took place. We attracted some attention and people asked us things like "Is this really going to happen?"

C.P. – That was hilarious. What I was trying to do was to create a situation, a myth, and people were willing to go along with it. In the U.S., I think, there is a kind of willingness to mythologize or romanticize things. You call your abandoned towns "ghost towns," while in England we just call them derelict.

C.A.M. – Well, then perhaps we could say that the phrase at the top of the plaques was the U.S. description of the landing, and the bottom lines made up the British version.

C.P. – That could be one way of thinking of it.

C.A.M. – The signs prompted an interesting range of responses. Some believed that the plaques were meant to be deliberately misleading. I believe you have said that people's own cynicism or levels of belief and disbelief are revealed when they confront your work.

C.P. – My work often provokes both strong like and dislike. I think anger or disbelief are just as good responses to my work as pleasure or delight. If I thought I was boring people then I would be sad.

C.A.M. – I wonder if it was like or dislike that motivated someone to remove one of the plaques from Leverett Pond. Did the thief just want it out of the park? Or is it hanging on his or her wall? I guess we'll never know.

C.P. – Well, it might reappear sometime. But I think it is great, the range of responses people have.

C.A.M. – Are you still pursuing your ambition to return a meteorite to space?

C.P. – Not actively at the moment, but often an idea will ferment for quite some time until the right opportunity presents itself to actually see it through.

Conversation between Nari Ward and Carole Anne Meehan about *Beautiful Necessity: Hugging Post*, Art on the Emerald Necklace, 3rd Annual ICA/Vita Brevis Project

Carole Anne Meehan – What drew you to the spot in Franklin Park that you used for your project?

Nari Ward – The ruins of the bear display felt like historic space, but neglected. I am often drawn to spaces that have been overlooked in some measure. Here were these glorious ruins that nobody seemed to know what to do with. Also, I felt a sense of nineteenth-century history that was specific to the period in which the park was conceived.

C.A.M. – So how did your sense of the park's mission influence your approach to the work?

N.W. – I was very interested in the notion of the park as an example of domesticated nature. It is a very charged space because of the wildness contained within a controlled, programmed space. There were a lot of contradictions that I was really interested in trying to work with. I began to think about both captivity and a sense of embrace.

C.A.M. – Would you elaborate?

N.W. – The thought behind *Hugging Post* was to play with the strange relationship between the idea of being embraced, but also being caught in a type of lock. It all depends upon the position one may hold in a close relationship, where one may feel a sense of competition or, instead, submission.

C.A.M. – It sounds like you may have been thinking in part about the experience of the animals who were kept here.

N.W. – Right, exactly. There was a primal thing about existence in general that I was trying to instill into the work, which is this notion of a "beautiful necessity." To me this is the need to be protected, but also at the same time, perhaps, to be in control. A "bear hug" could result in playful affection, or it could result in terror or confrontation. These dualities exist in any kind of zoo environment where an animal is kept under a certain amount of stress because it is not in its natural environment, but it is also protected.

C.A.M. – How did you develop your ideas for the piece's final form?

N.W. – I was fascinated by the large rusted cylinder that I found in the remnants of the bear cage. Cylinders such as these were placed around trees near the edge of the space and prevented the bears that were kept here from climbing and escaping from the display area. Trees were meant to be part of the bear's habitat, but the park managers obviously knew that they had to prevent the bears from escaping the enclosure.

C.A.M. – A very practical design solution.

N.W. – Yes. This collar that was created for the trees took the shape of a huge, metal shaft that sat above bars. I became interested in ways to transform, or isolate, this collar device. This was how I wanted to explore this idea of imprisonment versus a

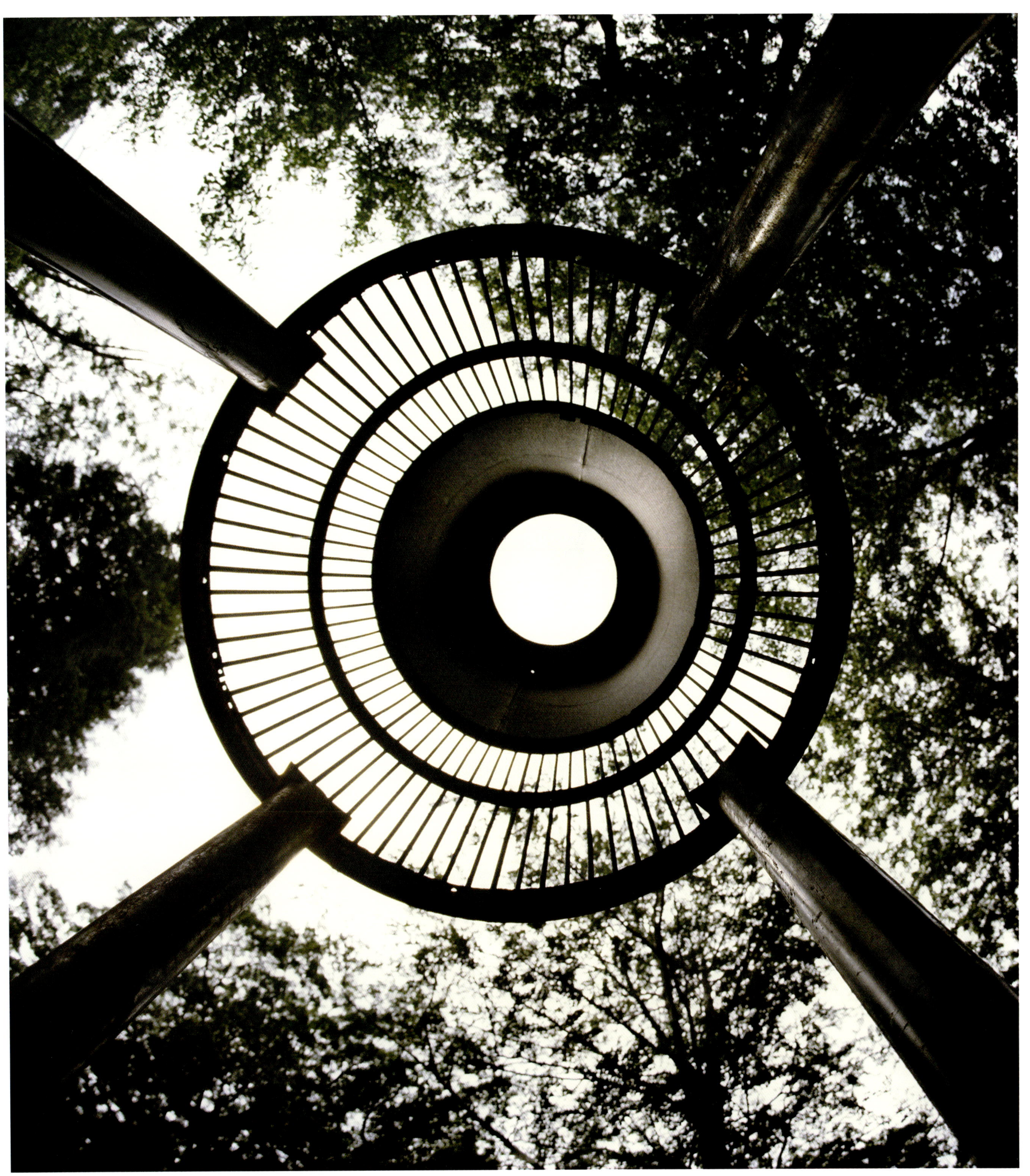

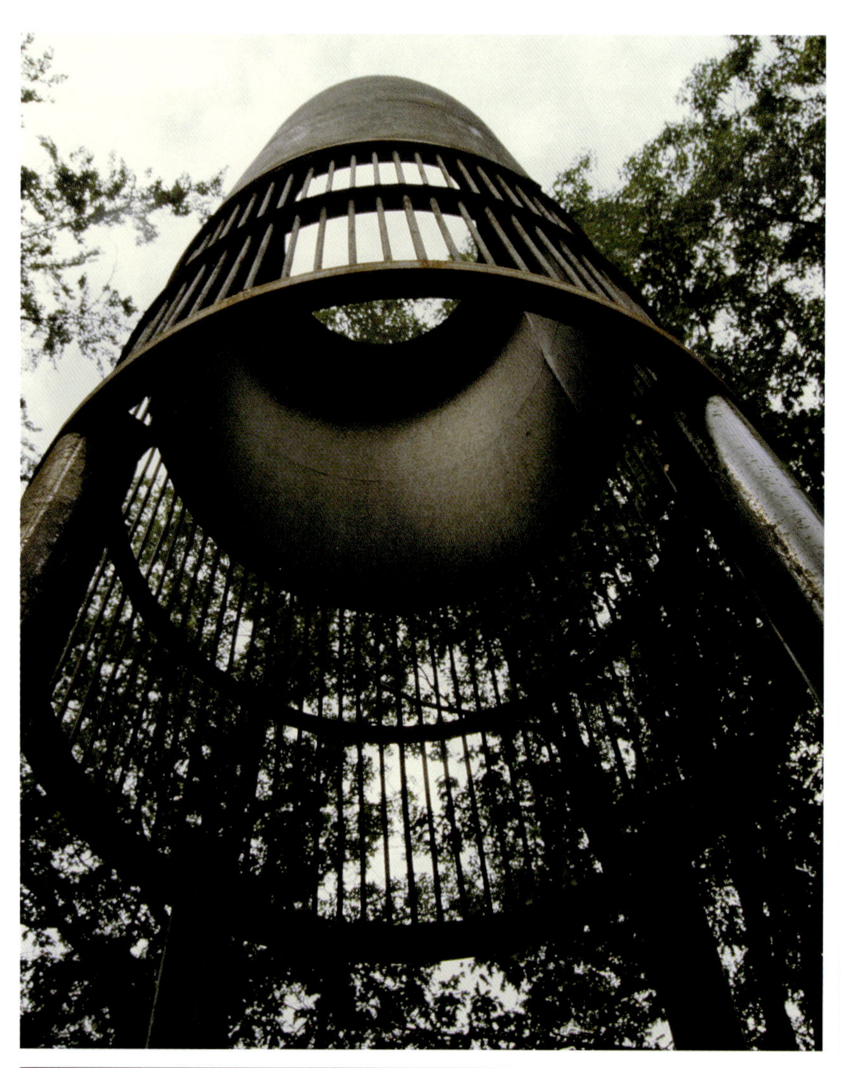

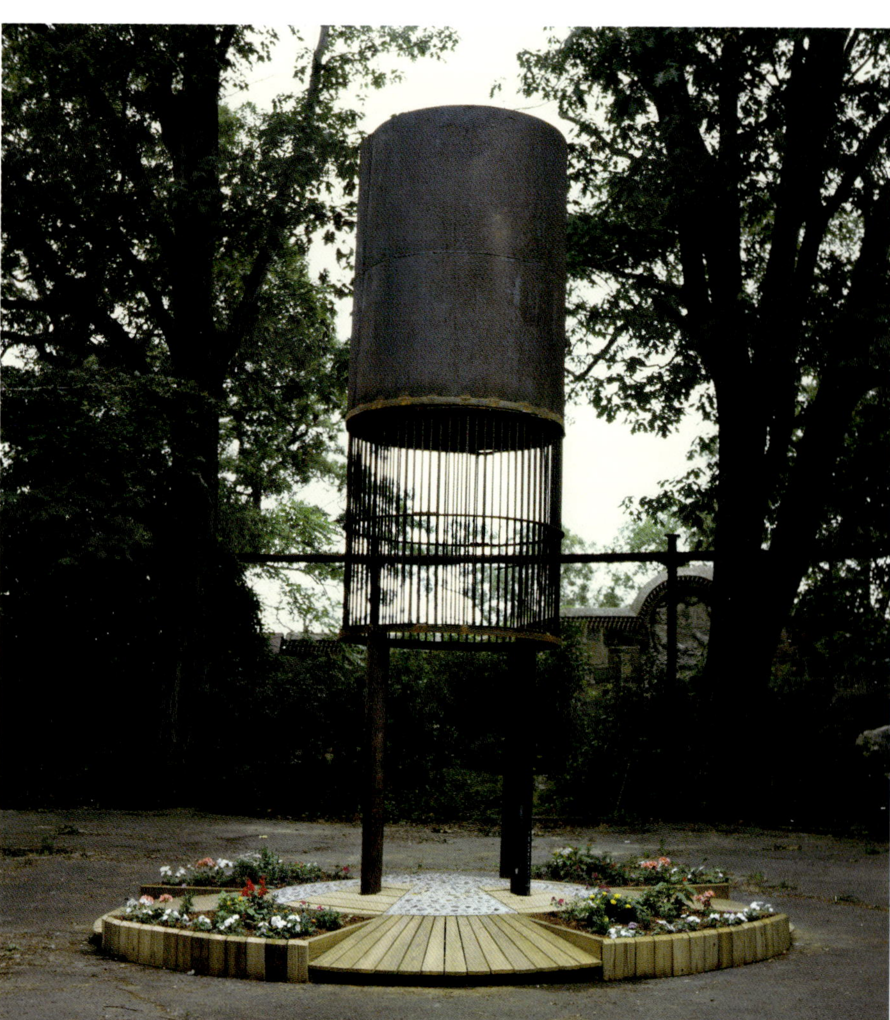

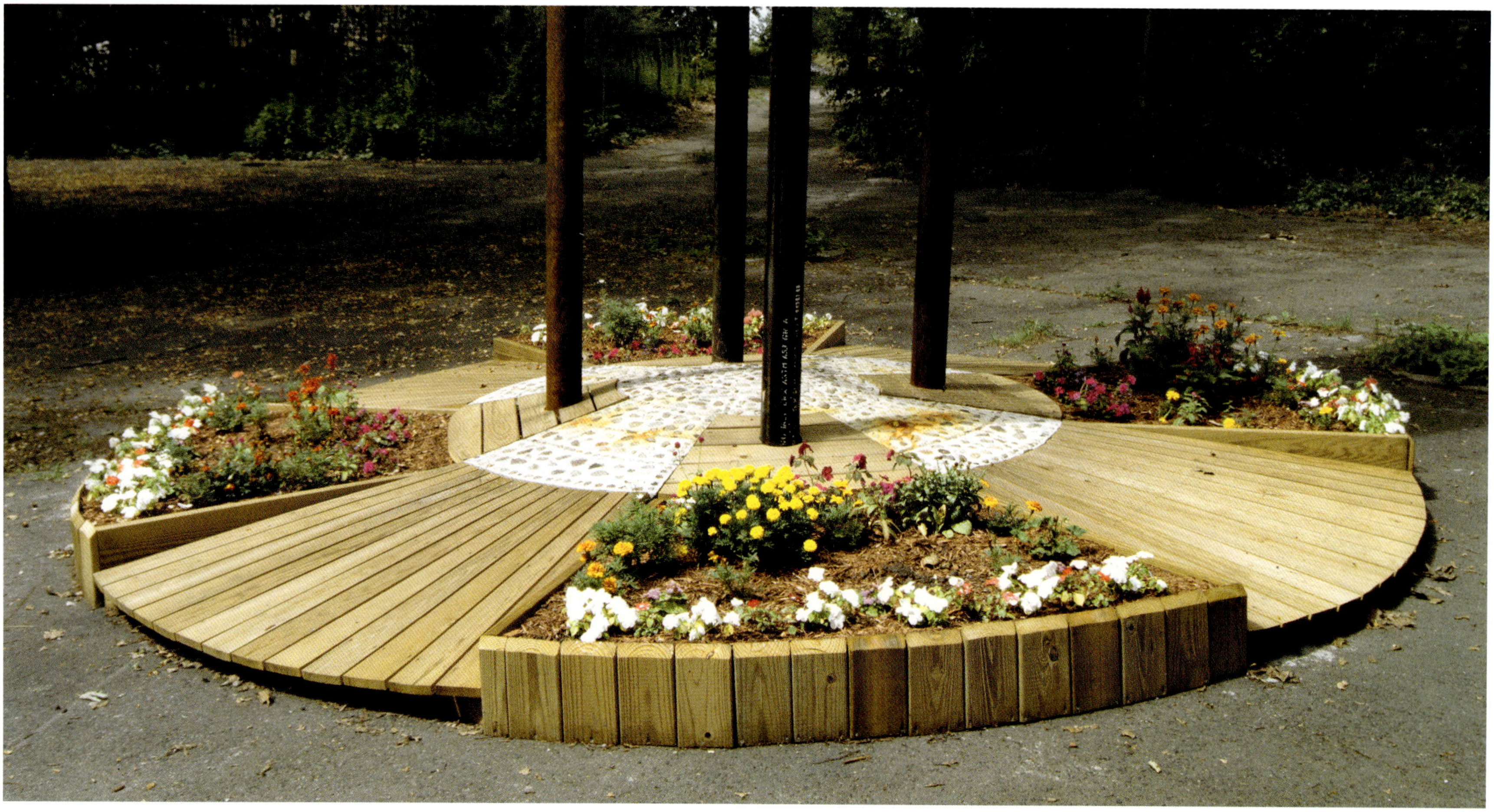

kind of protection. I felt this device was about both of those things. The tree is a part of nature, but in a formal park setting it ends up being somehow domesticated, controlled.

C.A.M. – The tower that you created from these elements, and the platform you set below it, seemed to be at once sheltering, but also exposing. While standing on this platform, but underneath the cylinder, you become more aware of your surroundings. In a sense you feel like you are on display, and sort of captured.

N.W. – It was really important that the platform be raised and sloped. When you walk up this slope you get the feeling of ascending, even though you are moving under the collar. I like the way this affects your experience of it spatially. A question I always ask when I go about making any kind of installation is, how do you make viewers more acutely aware of their presence, or of their own bodies? This seemed to be the way to do it in this instance.

C.A.M. – In this case the viewer assumes the position that the tree once held, too.

N.W. – Yes. I guess I was very interested in the tree's perspective. Unfortunately the tree was dead by the time I got there. It seems this collar limited the tree's potential for growth, which reinforces my ambivalence around attempts to rein nature in.

C.A.M. – How were you hoping to affect this area of the park with your project overall? Did you feel you succeeded in calling more attention to the park's domesticated wildness?

N.W. – The thing about art is that it can bring people into an underused area and give them the sense that it is looked after, cared for. It could lead to getting more people to come and experience it. It engaged my curiosity to use this space, perhaps just to see if my way of addressing the neglect might lead to more people using it. Maybe down the line something will happen to it in terms of improvements. The whole thing is just to get people to be more aware of parks in general, whether in a philosophical or social or political sense.

C.A.M. – Well certainly the tower was enough of an unusual object that people would wonder how it came to be there.

N.W. – Yes. It was about trying to create a visual contrast. The flowers and the stone patterns in the base provided a decorative contrast to the rugged cylinder. The collar was weighted with enough history that the addition of these decorative elements could lead the viewer to become more aware of everything else.

C.A.M. – The flower plantings and geometric platform were so sweet and orderly, and did give the feeling of this patch of land being tended to in the midst of all this overwhelming neglect. The design approach that you use here is quite opposite to the design principles that Olmsted used for the park overall.

N.W. – I did want the work to have a very different feel from the overall environment of the park. I wanted to find a way to have this thing be so out of place in order to create this other kind of space that could hold this wild object.

C.A.M. – *Beautiful Necessity* felt very urban. It could exist in Harlem, or in any rugged, urban center. In this sense you created another interesting contrast in that Franklin Park was Olmsted's attempt to create a sense of the countryside in the middle of the city. We often think of nature invading the urban environment if left to its own devices. Grass will push up through sidewalk cracks and so on. But your piece seemed to prove that the city will invade nature, too. The urban will not be beaten back, but will assert itself.

N.W. – The urban environment is so distinct from nature. This idea of the urban persists in the piece because this very physical object doesn't yield to the nature around it. It became a kind of hut or shelter that helps to set the space apart.

C.A.M. – It had a wonderful, improvised feel. It looked like the work of a master reclamation artist.

N.W. – I wanted to avoid overly designing the thing. I think it had its own unique presence that I wanted to preserve. We did very little to it, just adding reinforcements to make sure it wouldn't collapse. We left it in more sturdy shape than we found it.

C.A.M. – Looking straight up into the tower created quite a dramatic peephole.

N.W. – I wanted to create that effect, to isolate that moment when the viewer looks up. This ties in with my attempt to have the piece affect the feel of the space. I see Olmsted as a type of inspiration artist where his main concern was to get people to be aware of where they are. You know, getting them to realize that they are in a city, but that they are also in a special moment of being with nature.

Olafur Eliasson: *The young land*

The 4th Annual ICA/Vita Brevis Project
Summer 2001

Conversation between Olafur Eliasson and Carole Anne Meehan about *The young land,* 4th Annual ICA/Vita Brevis Project

Carole Anne Meehan – How did you arrive at the choice of using lava rock for this project? Was this the first time you used this material?

Olafur Eliasson – Yes, although I have used it since a couple of times. I was very interested in the potential for interactivity with the lava. I wanted a material, rocks or something, with an alien quality, especially that one would sense when walking on it. I wanted to use something that would give the feeling of physical displacement. I also thought it would create a nice contrast to an urban context–because of both the rock's tactile qualities, being this type of crunchy glass, and the meaning of lava–that could refer to a primordial state of nature that is very different from the seemingly static "here and now" urban context. Let's say the lava, although it's not really true, is the closest material that could be associated with the "big bang."

C.A.M. – At different times we talked about the purpose of the piece, what its function would be. You liked to think about it potentially as a park. At one point you talked about it being an island that would, in a way, address the shortage of land. Or it could be thought of as a viewing platform where you would have a whole different relationship to your body, and your position within the city, because of the uneven walking surface and the rocking motion of the barge. Do you think the piece fulfilled all of these things?

O.E. – While making a project you go through a process where ideas shift from one area to another. One is not more correct than another, but there is a progression where a set of ideas mutates and evolves. After the work was complete it became obvious to me that what particularly interested me was the idea of the relativity of space that the barge suggested. The different aspects that you mentioned came together in this broad idea that land is actually something you produce, that you generate. The "land" created by the piece could be an island, or land that could be mobile because it could float. I hope that the people who spent time on the barge sensed the possibility of these various ideas.

C.A.M. – And these ideas have an interesting relationship to the history of Boston, which largely sits on landfill.

O.E. – I am reluctant to put that reading on it, unless people are physically aware that Boston is built on a landfill, which I doubt. My experience is that people take things for granted as natural as they find them in their current state. They don't think of things like a city being built on landfill.

C.A.M. – People did bring their memories and notions of experience with lava.

O.E. – Yes, someone talked about it like being on the moon or on another planet.

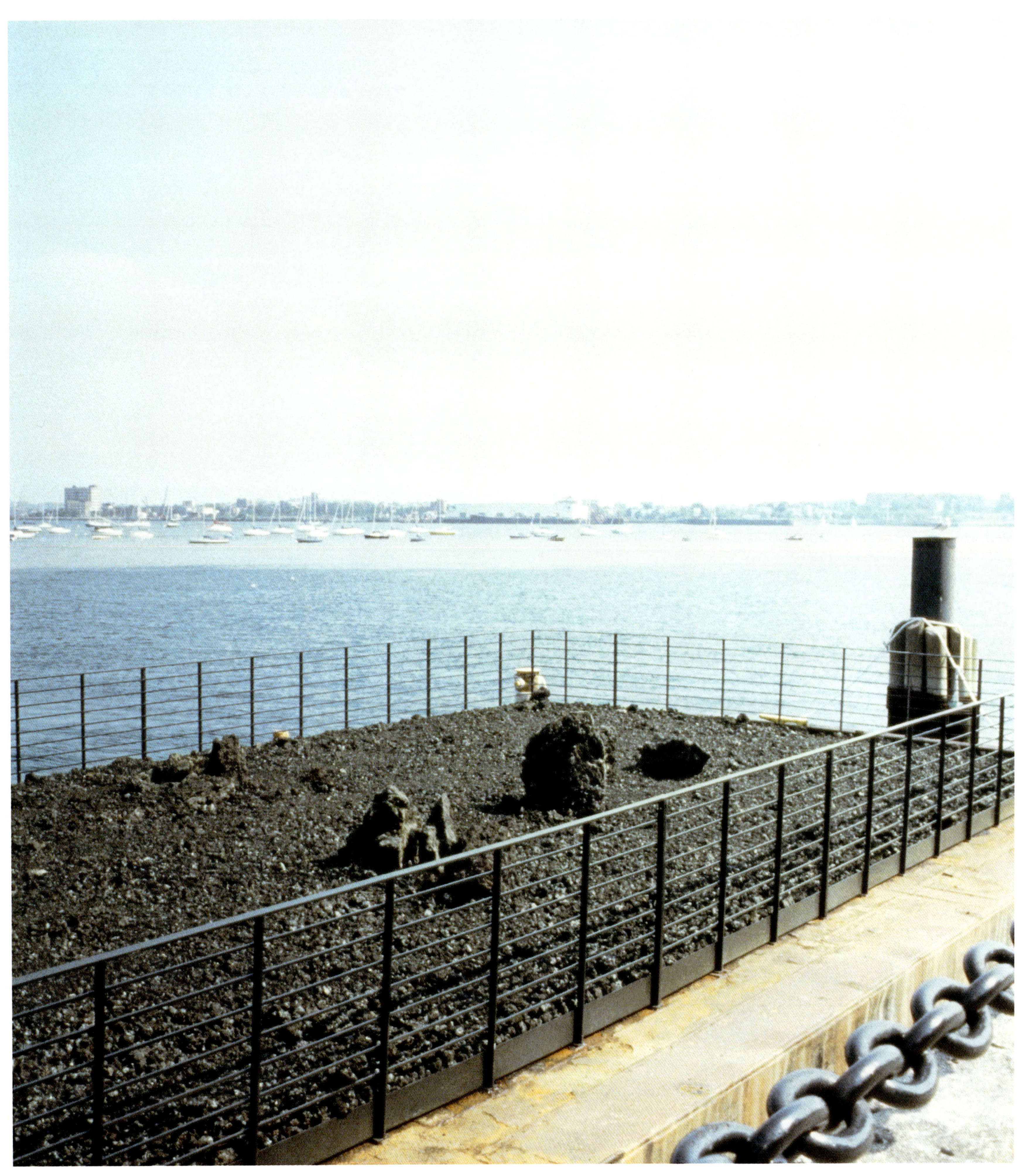

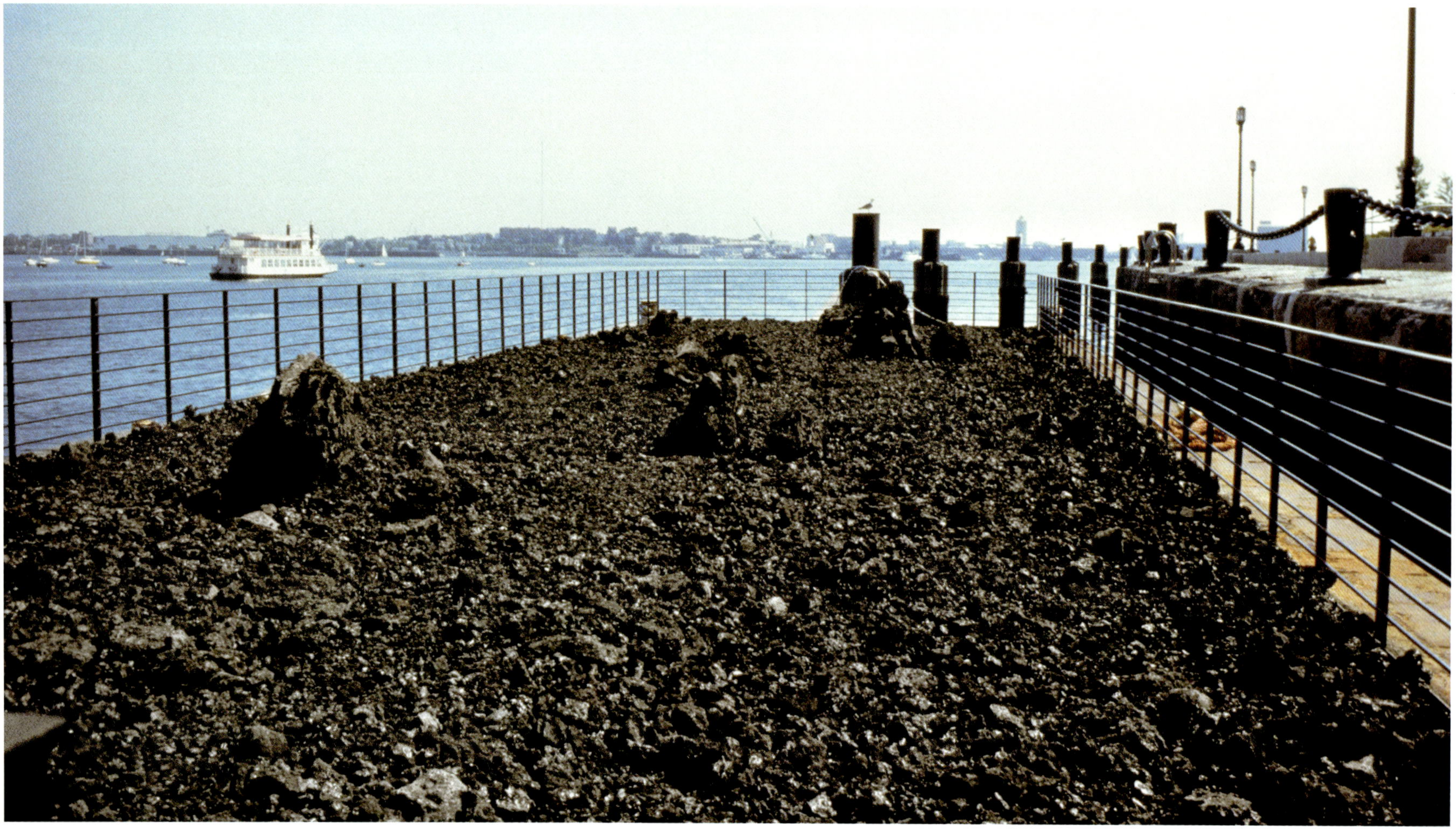

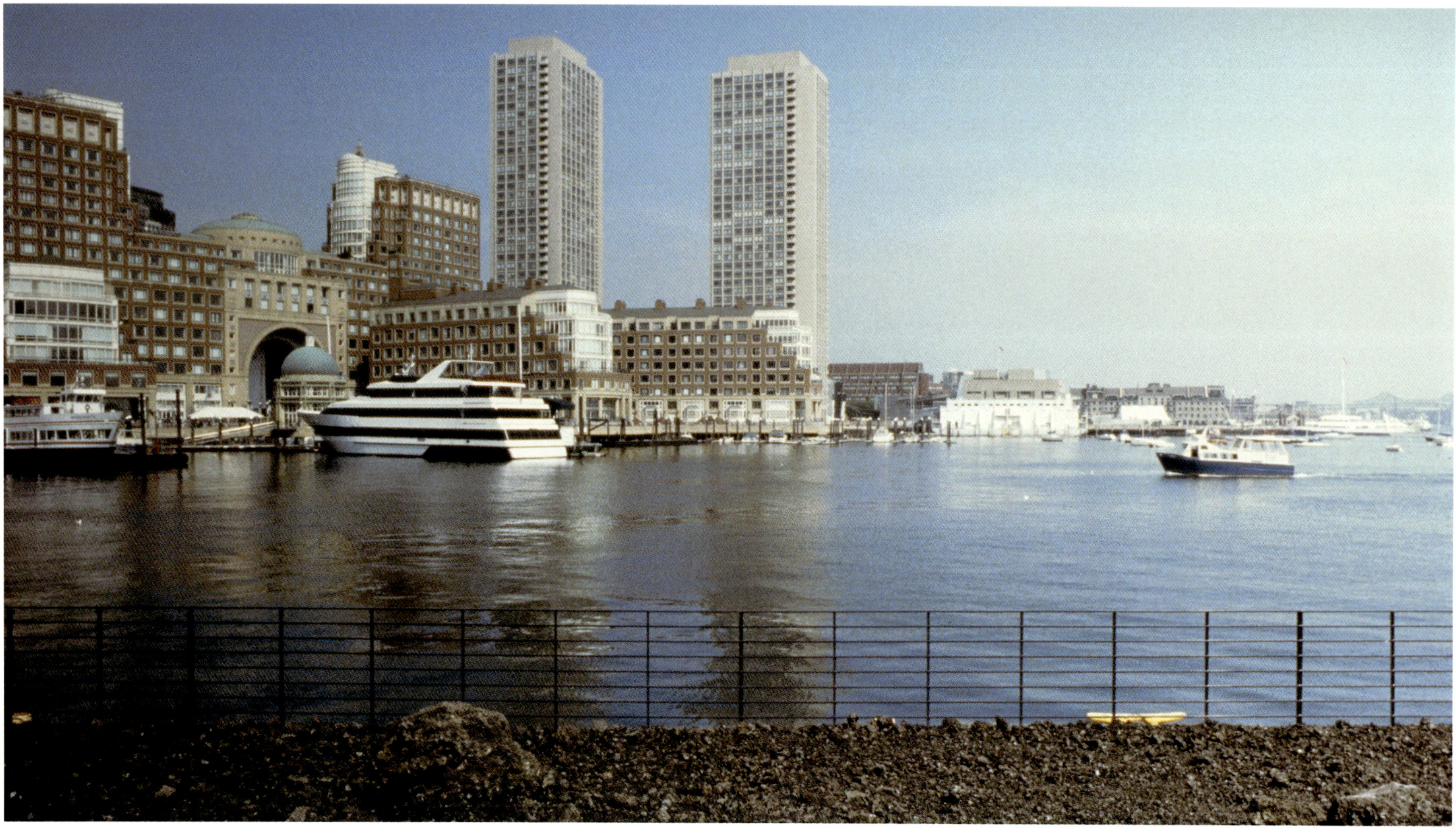

C.A.M. – *The young land* became a very interactive environment. People used the rocks to make mountains and hills. It became kind of an adult sandbox, which was really interesting.

O.E. – I am thrilled to know the project was used like that, which was a central idea from the beginning. In museums there are always ideas about archiving and conservation and not allowing people to touch paintings and so on. But in a work where you actually want people to interact physically, it is difficult to let people know that this is welcomed without becoming patronizing. But then there is the chance the public will alter the experience of the piece too much. There is a weird balance in this situation that needs to be achieved.

C.A.M. – Yes, it is true. After not seeing the project for a couple of weeks I was struck by how many of these big and little mountains had been made with piled-up rocks. We would have to adjust them so they wouldn't tip.

O.E. – I have more problems with people who are so humble and polite, and are just very thankful if they can even walk on a project.

C.A.M. – You have often said that a work of art should not be more important than the person looking at it.

O.E. – Yes. The so-called correct way of behaving in museums supposedly gives one a higher understanding of the goings-on in museums. I think it would be important to propose a platform where a certain amount of self-reflection is actually possible. People would evaluate what they see, the painting or the lava or whatever, but they also would evaluate their own protocol as they go about seeing things. In my opinion, museums have a responsibility to encourage people to evaluate how they see.

C.A.M. – Let's talk about *The young land*'s aesthetic characteristics. The project had a wonderfully grand humility, with the incredible rustiness of the barge and the dark color of the rocks blending in. When we talked about locations for the project we had hoped to secure some rugged, outlying areas. I see it as fortunate that we ended up close to Boston's more polished downtown, which provided a visual contrast to all of this ruggedness. Otherwise the piece might have just blended too much into the scenery.

O.E. – Yes, but a more subtle context would also have been good. A higher degree of intimacy would have been beneficial for other aspects of the piece that we, in the location we used, were less able to understand. Then again, being in front of the big courthouse and close to the quite sleek downtown provided other meanings.

C.A.M. – Would you talk about some of these meanings?

O.E. – The downtown architecture represents the skeletons of what is left of the modern dream, what is thought of as "the good life." To me these are very odd palaces, such as hotels, shopping arcades, the courthouse, and so on. There is this urge to hold on to some arcane notions of what is beautiful and what is a good-looking building. The barge could be a metaphor for industrialization that was the beginning of this modern dream.

C.A.M. – At one point you considered building walls for the barge with a reflective surface on the inside. You have used reflection very effectively in some of your other works. But then you opted for the open rail design, which provided a subtle frame for the lava bed.

O.E. – Again, there is always a range of ideas that you go through when conceiving a piece. The idea of the reflective surface was just one. I was thinking I could make the area holding the lava look bigger, more expansive. I finally realized that *The young land* was a much more conceptual project than a decorative, visually flashy one. So I decided to minimize it down to a few straightforward components.

C.A.M. – Have you thought about doing more projects in public settings, away from institutional settings?

O.E. – Yes, all of the time. For me it is important to reinforce the understanding that the potential of the museum lays not in the white cube, but in the dialogue between the white cube and the city. The power of public pieces such as this is that they question and upend the museum's static location and dependence on the white cube. There is a value to these sorts of projects that are not predetermined, where people would just walk by and say, "Oh, what is this?" as they wander through the city. These provide a way to restore activity and compassion to an urban environment, and integrate people into the life of the city.

C.A.M. – It is reassuring to hear you say these things. But we do struggle with how to measure the impact of these outlying projects on audiences.

O.E. – Letting go of these concerns is not part of the accepted museum protocol that I was talking about earlier. But there is a value in letting go that we might not see. There is a certain value in actually saying that we have a society where there is a space for letting go.

Ann Carlson and Mary Ellen Strom: *Remedy*

The 5th Annual ICA/Vita Brevis Project
May 2003

Conversation between Ann Carlson, Mary Ellen Strom, and Carole Anne Meehan about *Remedy*, 5th Annual ICA/Vita Brevis Project

Carole Anne Meehan – The ICA gave you the enormous, and most likely impossible, task of creating a public work that investigates notions of art and healing within a hospital context. You must love a challenge. Why didn't you tell us to go away and leave you alone?

Ann Carlson – I did originally.

C.A.M. – You did? (Laughs.) I guess I missed that.

A.C. – I thought it would be too close for comfort in terms of my own experiences with my children. I thought about working in Children's Hospital, but also felt I didn't want to know about all of the things that can go wrong. I then thought about looking at all kinds of institutions centered on health and healing within an urban environment, but after 9/11 I became more intrigued with public health. So for several months we asked for informational interviews in public health offices. This was partly driven by the anthrax scare in New York post 9/11.

C.A.M. – We did have a number of meetings right after September 11. Are you willing to talk about how 9/11 affected your thinking about the project?

A.C. – Oh sure. I was emotionally traumatized, and a bit wiped out. It was as though my personal hard drive was gone. I questioned why bother to make work? I had a depressed, blank feeling. So I was hoping these informational interviews would help me to get kick-started again.

C.A.M. – Did these interviews give you a kick-start or help to restore anything?

A.C. – It restored a sense of "Oh, here are these people who are taking care of these infrastructures." I felt encouraged and inspired. A few of the people we met were former political activists and extremely committed. They were there because of compassion and concern for the health of the community. I was reminded that people have a drive of compassion and concern and commitment.

C.A.M. – It was pretty overwhelming. What they deal with in a day is somewhat in the background because it deals with abstractions and statistics.

A.C. – We heard about many statistics and information and results. It was a smorgasbord of information. In a way it was overwhelming and in another way it was very reaffirming.

C.A.M. – Some of the people we met with were interesting in that they had the experience of working in the public health and statistical arena but also with patients one-on-one. The people who were able to strike that kind of balance between the personal and the abstract were pretty inspiring to talk to.

A.C. – It was confusing to make connections constantly between the individual and the wider community. Flipping back and forth from anecdotal, personal information to hearing

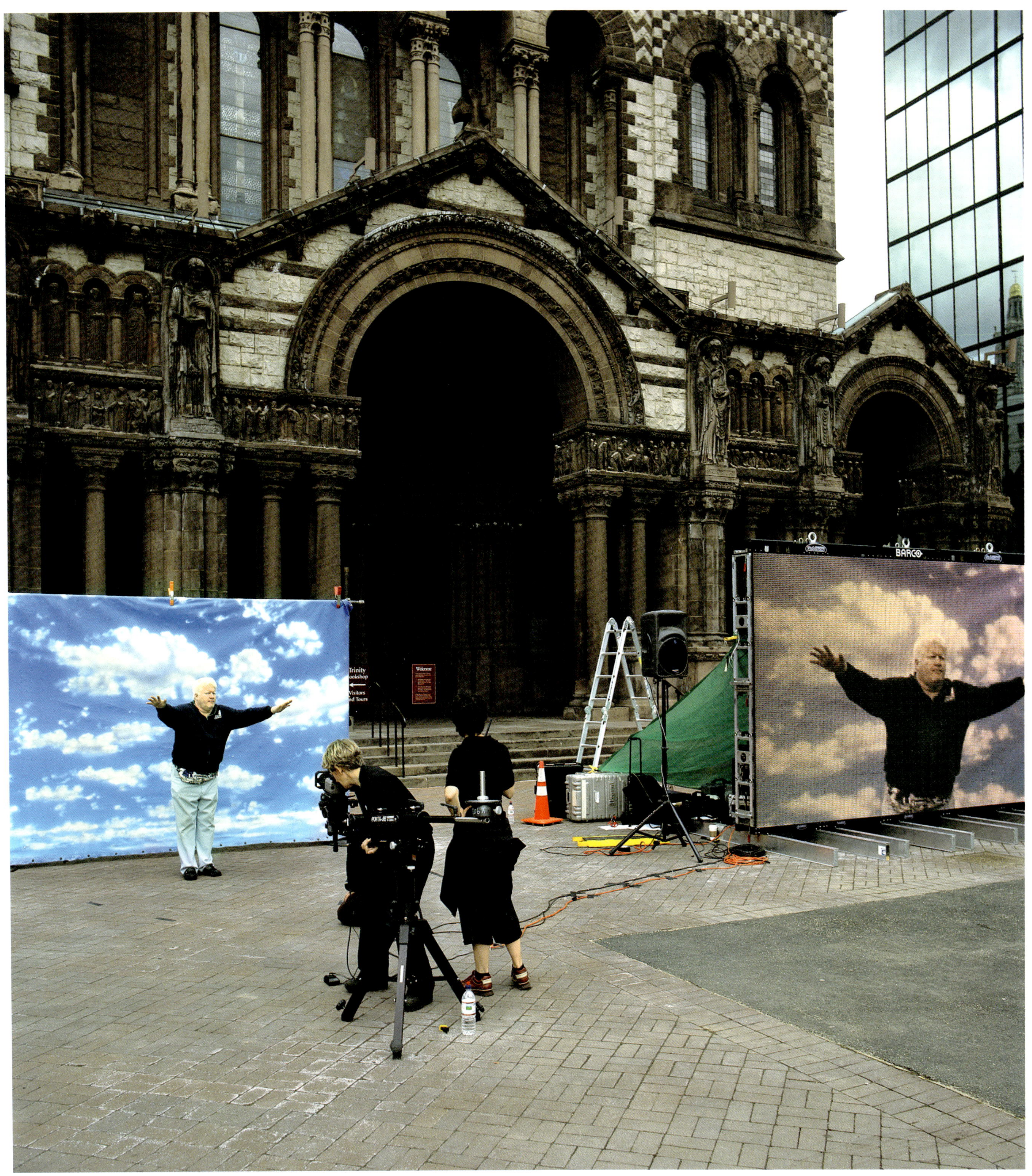
Trinity
Welcome
BARCO

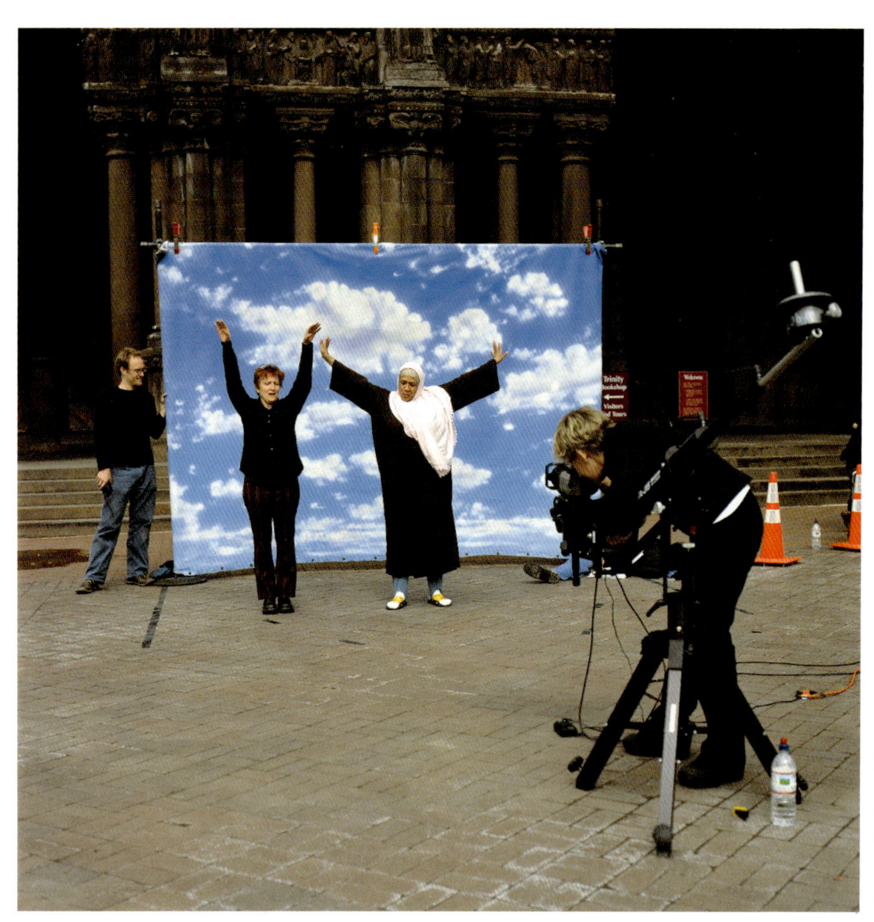

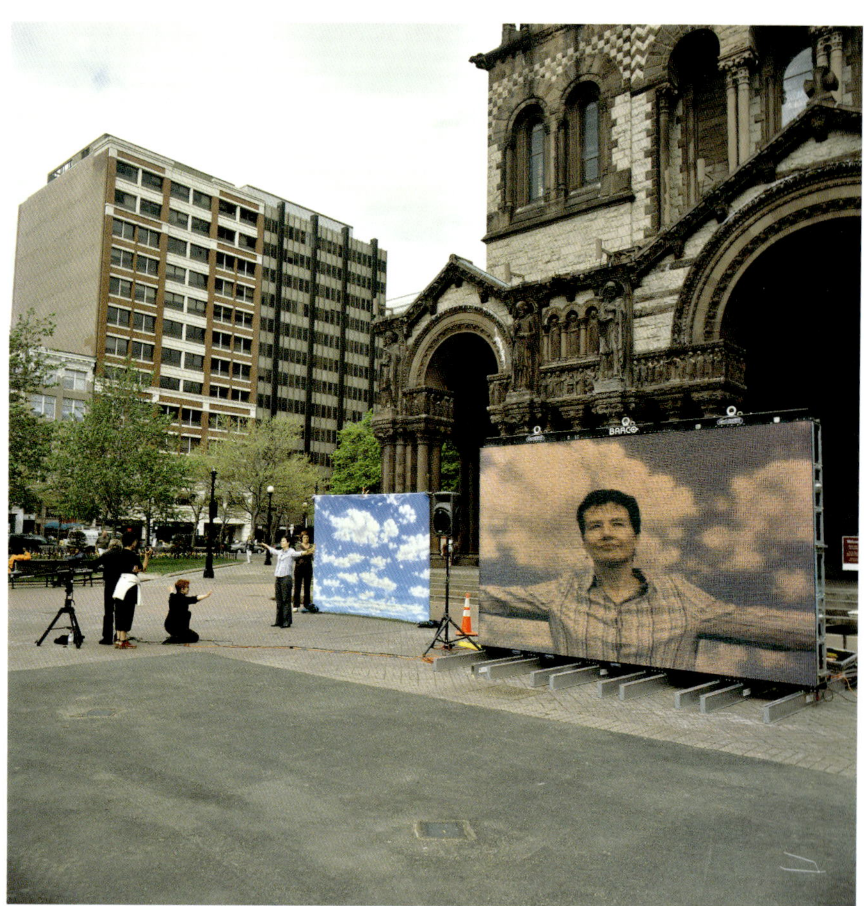

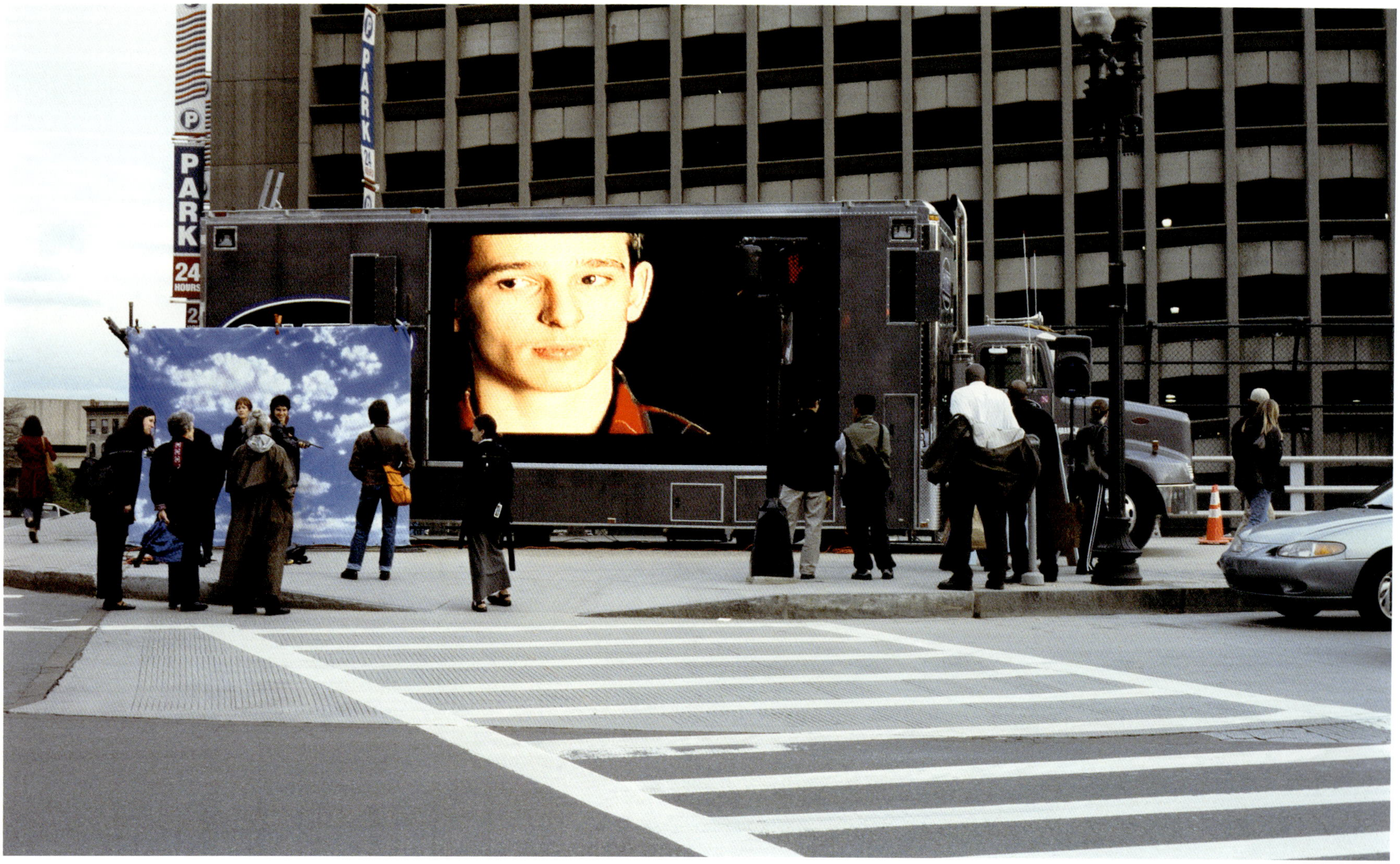

about broader impacts. I wondered how I would narrow this information down, and how it would fit into the concept and structure for the work we would ultimately create.

C.A.M. – Well, then let's talk about how a shape for the final work began to emerge. How did you prepare to videotape the doctors and other medical professionals?

Mary Ellen Strom – We had a significant, practical problem to solve, which was figuring out how to make a time-based work with people who don't have a lot of time. This was a driving issue that arose from working with doctors and public-health professionals. And how to take all of that post-9/11 anxiety, and the anxiety that was building around the impending war in Iraq. How would we materialize this in a nonverbal form?

A.C. – It was not just about how busy the doctors were, but how important, in my mind and in a hierarchical way, someone's time is.

C.A.M. – Yes, they deal daily with matters of life and death and here we are knocking at their door.

M.E.S. – It was important to respect the limits on their time and to figure out how to work very deeply and intensely within these limitations. This actually became fuel for the final form of the production.

A.C. – The time constraints ended up being a good thing. I was extremely welcomed by the doctors once I pushed through my own hesitation about taking up their valuable time. The production studio became a real leveler. Everybody was very focused and prepared and ready to give it his or her best during taping.

C.A.M. – They probably also appreciated a moment when they were pulled out of their demanding day.

M.E.S. – What Ann and I do together requires an incredible focus and flow where we are working improvisationally, in the moment. We know we have just this one chance of getting it. There is a lot of trust between us. I think they also experienced that trust.

C.A.M. – That was very clear to the few who had the privilege of observing you at work.

A.C. – We were inviting people into this other way of thinking and moving. Looking back, I see it was almost a meditation. At times it was a kind of performance. Something happened in that time because of that trust Mary Ellen was talking about, but also as a result of my hours and hours spent observing the people, having some knowledge of what their work life was like.

M.E.S. – The performers–the medical people–had a lot of power in this situation, too. They would know when we got the take, because they had to do their part with commitment. I had to do it right and Ann had to direct them correctly. It was a three-part improvisation. There was a coming together of movement from their day, put together in a sequence. They were really working choreographically with the camera.

A.C. – I think one of the things I found depressing is that part of a doctor's life is to "perform" in order to convince a patient to have confidence in him or her. With us they had a willingness to be vulnerable.

C.A.M. – It must have been a very welcome shift. What was it like to shadow the doctors?

A.C. – It was very profound for me. I found it very complex in terms of thinking about the methods of Western medicine.

M.E.S. – And it must have something to do with the doctor you want to be.

A.C. – Yes, I have always wanted to go to medical school. I don't know if I would want to be a practicing physician but I have always had the desire to have the information. It is not a big leap to being an artist who uses a body all of the time to wanting to know everything about the body, its operating systems and so on. No pun intended.

C.A.M. – That is an interesting parallel.

A.C. – So I was there as a sponge. What did I know? What didn't I know? I had some amazing conversations with different practitioners who were thinking about their work within a broader cultural context. What does it mean to be a doctor in 2003? What does it mean to be a healer today?

C.A.M. – I know it is not your favorite term, but was the word "healing" used much?

A.C. – No, never.

C.A.M – Well, to shift gears here, the score that you chose by Lauren Weinger was very haunting. You had a few different ideas about how sound would be used.

A.C. – It was partially serendipitous. I have always admired Lauren's work. After my brother died she sent me a piece of music along with a book. It was a number of weeks before I listened to it. It just seemed really right.

M.E.S. – Lauren gave it to you as a gift when your brother died and it was very moving to you. There is a part of *Remedy* that attempts to address mortality in a way that helps us look at our humanness and humanity. And I think that her intention with that piece was to address that.

C.A.M. – So it really is a requiem. Did it have a title?

M.E.S. – *Bells #1.* I have worked with Lauren for many years so I was confident that she would understand the intention of *Remedy*, and also be able to enliven or activate the piece in an outdoor context.

C.A.M. – Her piece is complex. At a certain point it really builds and almost feels like it is going to explode. To shift things again, I have some questions about the video editing of *Remedy*. We have talked quite a bit about how the filming was a collaborative process. Did you also hit deep levels of collaboration during editing?

A.C. – I got kind of blank during the edit. I went back to my earlier state of hard-drive meltdown, although I had a really clear image in my mind about how these movement-based portraits should look. But I mostly handed it all over to Mary Ellen. It is her medium. Although I would come back and say, for example, this is Iris and most of the time she is typing. It seems to be about her fingernails, although it is not just about her fingernails.

M.E.S. – My strategy was to find the individual shots that really spoke about what I knew about that person. I worked very minimally to keep it as simple as possible. I wanted their non-verbal-based communication to be in the foreground, and not be muddled through any type of digital processing.

C.A.M. – At one point you had talked about using some software to manipulate the images.

M.E.S. – That was an idea that fell by the wayside. This was a very interesting and unusual experience for me because my approach is normally more analytical and critical. This was a chance to work very intuitively.

C.A.M. – Let's talk about the public presentation. We had the piece in three distinct settings. For part of it the truck was mobile around the hospital district with the screen active. And then it sat on a sidewalk across from the ICA exhibition opening. And then for two days we located it in a public plaza in the heart of the city.

A.C. – The truck was fantastic, with this commercial kind of context meeting a fine-art context.

C.A.M. – What about the experience of doing the "on the spot" portraits in the park? You were all of a sudden creating work with people you hadn't met. How did you condense the process?

A.C. – I didn't know there would be so many volunteers. It turned out we couldn't do all of the people who wanted to do it. One of the things I like doing best in life is asking someone to "come on over and do this movement, now do this one." In this circumstance it was an immediate, intuitive read. I felt a little like a psychic, not unlike the tradition of on-the-spot palm reading or something. I would talk to the person a little bit and from there develop three or four ideas.

C.A.M. – On which you could build?

A.C. – Yes. Sometimes he or she would decide to have Mary Ellen's camera go close-up on the face. Their choice would be in service to him or her being visible in another kind of way, as a metaphor for being a citizen. The person becomes both fully himself or herself, and also part of something bigger.

M.E.S. – If we had done this five years ago issues of privacy would have arisen. Today surveillance is very common in our society. People are so used to getting their picture taken that they are perhaps more comfortable when a camera is present than not. They believe their mediated, repeated image gives them authority. Celebrities or people who hold power–we look at their picture again and again and again. Ordinary people have a lot of desire to be in front of the camera. I would say it becomes about fulfilling that desire and giving people the power of visibility.

A.C. – It was really amazing how much they enjoyed it. Perhaps we should set up cameras in town squares everywhere.

Artists' Biographies
by Emily Moore, Curatorial Assistant

Shimon Attie
Born 1957 in Los Angeles, California. Lives and works in New York City.

Shimon Attie sheds light upon the hidden histories embedded in the architecture of the present. Attie gained prominence through a series of European public projects he completed between 1991 and 1996, which explored the history of World War II, Jewish life, and the Holocaust. For *The Writing on the Wall* (1991–1993) Attie projected pre-World War II photographs of residents of Berlin's Jewish neighborhood onto the locations where the originals were taken. He has completed similarly poetic and haunting works in Cologne, Copenhagen, Dresden, Amsterdam, and Krakow. His first site-specific project in the United States, *Between Dreams and History* (1998), investigated the rich history of New York City's Lower East Side. Attie interviewed the neighborhood's residents, collecting memories and experiences of the neighborhood. He then wove these into a text that was projected with lasers onto building façades. Attie was a fellow at the American Academy in Rome from 2001–2002 where he projected images of Roman Jewish inhabitants onto ruins. Attie has had solo exhibitions at the Institute of Contemporary Art, Boston; the Cleveland Museum of Art; and the Museum of Contemporary Photography, Chicago. He has received fellowships from the National Endowment for the Arts, the Pollock-Krasner Foundation, and the Kunstfonds in Germany.

James Boorstein
Born 1955 in New York City. Lives and works in New York City.

In the mid-1980s, James Boorstein became disenchanted with the art world and traditional modes of making art and began creating work outside the normal studio context. Over the past twenty years his work has included night photography, video, site-specific sculpture, and installations that play with notions of perception and place. His work calls attention to the subtle and unnoticed, inviting viewers to take a closer look at their surroundings. For *Spirit of Place*, a 1998 group exhibition of site-specific sculpture in Huntington, Vermont, he created a musical staff between two ancient oak trees using shimmering audio tape. In another piece he created a gossamer blue mist using ultra-thin thread in a horizontal band around three young pine trees. Boorstein is currently writing a book that chronicles a series of contemplative walks around the outermost edge of Manhattan. The artist has had solo exhibitions at Southern Vermont College, Bennington, Vermont; St. Clement's Gallery, New York, New York; and Cité Internationale des Arts, Paris. He is the recipient of the American Center, Paris Residency Fellowship and the Helene Wurlitzer Foundation's Residency Fellowship in Taos, New Mexico. In 2002, Boorstein was a fellow at the MacDowell Colony in Peterborough, New Hampshire.

Ann Carlson
Born 1954 in Evanston, Illinois. Lives and works in New York City.

Performance artist and choreographer Ann Carlson often subverts conventional notions of dance–the use of classically trained dancers and traditional choreography. In 1986, Carlson presented "Sloss, Kerr, Rosenberg, and Moore," a nine-minute dance performed by four lawyers. Carlson based their movements, which humorously highlighted the high level of stress associated with their profession, on the group's real-life gestures and daily routines. This performance marked the beginning of Carlson's *Real People* series, an ongoing project featuring people bound by shared interests, activities, or relationships. In addition to lawyers the series has included nuns, security guards, museum professionals, fly fishers, and more. *Real People* illustrates Carlson's interest in uncovering beauty, dance, and movement in the subtle and the everyday. Her series *Animals*, which toured internationally to widespread acclaim, consisted of five dances that incorporated live animals performing as themselves. For her *Night Light* series, which has taken place in six U.S. cities, Carlson restages historical photographs in the manner of *tableaux vivant*. Carlson has received many grants and awards including several fellowships in choreography from the National Endowment for the Arts; the CalArts/Alpert Award in the Arts; and a Guggenheim Fellowship in choreography.

Ellen Driscoll

Born 1955 in Boston, Massachusetts. Lives and works in Cambridge, Massachusetts, and New York City.

Ellen Driscoll's multimedia work includes quiet, subtle drawings, sculptures, and large-scale public projects. Her subject matter is varied, examining both universal themes and personal history. As travelers scurry between subways and trains in New York City's Grand Central Terminal North they may pause to notice Driscoll's striking permanent installation, *As Above, So Below*. Completed in 1999, the work consists of twenty-one glass mosaics depicting the night sky of five different continents, produced using traditional mosaic techniques combined with digital technology. Driscoll's exhibition and performance, *Ahab's Wife, or the Whale* (1998), which explored the notion of a divided body, was inspired by her father's experience of a stroke that paralyzed half of his body, and by Herman Melville's description of the whale in *Moby Dick*. Driscoll has had solo exhibitions at the Massachusetts College of Art; The Contemporary Arts Center, Cincinnati; and the Whitney Museum of American Art at Philip Morris, New York. She has received numerous awards and fellowships including a Guggenheim Fellowship; a Bunting Institute Fellowship; and two fellowships in sculpture from the National Endowment for the Arts.

Olafur Eliasson

Born 1967 in Copenhagen, Denmark. Lives and works in Berlin, Germany.

While constructed through rather simple and straightforward means, Olafur Eliasson's sculptures and installations have awe inspiring and thrilling effects. Eliasson invites viewers into unexpected and engaging situations, which allow for contemplation of time, space, nature, and science. Eliasson's works are linked through their power to challenge perceptions about our natural and unnatural surroundings. His diverse output has included a ring of fire on a gallery wall, a floor of ice in a museum in Brazil, an artificial sunset in The Netherlands, a steam geyser outside of a museum in Pittsburgh, and a stunning series of photographic works that track and map the geological landscape of Iceland. Eliasson has had solo exhibitions at the Institute of Contemporary Art, Boston; the Center for Art and Media, Karlsruhe, Germany; Musée d'Art Moderne de la Ville de Paris; the Kunsthaus Bregenz, Austria; and the Irish Museum of Modern Art, Dublin. His work has appeared in numerous international art exhibitions including the Carnegie International 1999/2000, Pittsburgh, Pennsylvania, and the Venice Biennale in 2003. Also in 2003 Eliasson created an installation entitled *The Weather Project* for the Turbine Hall of the Tate Modern in London to great, worldwide acclaim.

Barnaby Evans

Born 1953 in Berkeley, California. Lives and works in Providence, Rhode Island.

In 1994, Barnaby Evans first presented *WaterFire*, a public art project staged on the three rivers of Providence, Rhode Island, to commemorate the 10th anniversary of First Night Providence. Three years later, due to immense community support and enthusiasm for the project, *WaterFire* became an ongoing multimedia event. This powerful celebration of water, fire, music, urban life, and people has been integral to the revitalization of downtown Providence. Barnaby Evans is also known for his museum installations including *Rikyu's Second Dream*, at the Rhode Island School of Design Museum of Art in 1999. This project was inspired by Sen Rikyu, the creator of the Japanese tea ceremony. Evans's photography is included in the collections of the Victoria and Albert Museum, London; the Addison Gallery of American Art, Andover, Massachusetts; and the Bibliotheque National, Paris. In 2000 Evans was awarded an Honorary Doctorate of Humanities by Brown University and an Honorary Doctorate of Fine Arts by Rhode Island College. He received the Aaron Siskind Fellowship in Photography and Providence's Renaissance Award in 1997. In 2003, Evans received the Kevin Lynch Award from the Massachusetts Institute of Technology Department of Urban Studies and Planning.

Jim Hodges

Born 1957 in Spokane, Washington. Lives and works in New York City.

Jim Hodges's work is deceptively simple and unabashedly visually appealing. His sculptures and installations evoke a wide range of associations, often conveying a certain sense of nostalgia and optimism. In 1994 Jim Hodges exhibited *A Diary of Flowers*, an installation of 565 drawings of flowers on paper napkins. This show introduced audiences to Hodges's ability to find beauty and order in the momentary, the humble, and the unexpected. He employs commonplace materials such as artificial flowers, chains, and mirrors, transforming them into stunning curtains of sewn flowers, spider webs of delicate chains, and canvases composed with broken mirrors. Music and sound have informed and shaped Hodges's recent work, including *Subway Music Box* (2000), a video piece that weaves together the sights and sounds of twenty-four New York City subway musicians, and *colorsound* (2003), an installation at the Addison Gallery of American Art in North Andover, Massachusetts, exploring the visual quality of sound and the sound of color. Hodges has had one-person exhibitions at the Kemper Museum of Contemporary Art, Kansas City, Missouri; the Museum of Contemporary Art, Chicago; and the Institute of Contemporary Art, Boston. His work is in the permanent collections of the Museum of Modern Art in New York; the Whitney Museum of American Art; the Guggenheim Museum in New York; the Art Institute of Chicago; the San Francisco Museum of Modern Art; the Los Angeles County Museum of Art; and the Pompidou Center in Paris.

Mildred Howard

Born 1945 in San Francisco, California. Lives and works in San Francisco.

As a child growing up in San Francisco in the 1950s, Mildred Howard's parents, who ran an antiques shop, were very active in both the civil rights movement and community politics. The influence of Howard's youth can be seen in her work, which reflects a rich mixture of the historical, the contemporary, the political, and the familial. Her sculptures and installations frequently incorporate found objects that are ripe with meaning. These reference Howard's explorations of African American history and critical meditations on class and gender. She has completed a series of sculptures using Billie Holiday records, as well as a group of works incorporating mammy or Aunt Jemima figurines. Her installation, *In the Line of Fire*, which included fifteen life-size World War I soldiers based on a photograph of a cousin, spoke to the often overlooked service of African Americans in the United States military. Howard's work has been exhibited at many museums and galleries including The City Gallery, Leicester, England; the Berkeley Art Center, Berkeley, California; and the San Jose Museum of Art, San Jose, California. Her work is included in the collections of the Miami Dade Public Library, Miami, Florida; the Wadsworth Atheneum, Hartford, Connecticut; and the Oakland Museum, Oakland, California. Howard has been included in recent editions of *Jansen's History of Art*.

Kennedy & Violich Architecture

Sheila Kennedy, born 1957 in Chicago, Illinois.
Frano Violich, born 1957 in San Francisco, California.
Both live and work in Boston, Massachusetts.

Sheila Kennedy and Frano Violich founded Kennedy & Violich Architecture, an inter-disciplinary architectural practice, in 1988. Their services range from urban and architectural design to material design and development. According to Kennedy and Violich, their practice "explores new possibilities for a contemporary public architecture and urbanism," blurring boundaries between fine art and architecture. In addition to architectural commissions, they produce installations and site-specific work for museums. Their projects have included private residences, buildings for schools and colleges, libraries, ferry terminals, and public bathrooms. Their clients have included the School of the Art Institute of Chicago, the Rhode Island School of Design, Harvard University, the City of New York, and the Boston Center for the Arts. Their work has been shown in exhibitions at the Museum of Modern Art, New York; San Francisco Museum of Modern Art; the Wexner Center for the Arts, Columbus, Ohio; and the Massachusetts Museum of Contemporary Art. Kennedy & Violich Architecture has received three design excellence awards from the Boston Society of Architects, three National Honor Awards for Design from the American Institute of Architects, and two Progressive Architecture Awards. They were selected by the Architectural League of New York as young American architects who have made a significant contribution to architecture in the public realm.

Cornelia Parker
Born 1956 in Cheshire, England. Lives and works in London, England.

Through her artwork, Cornelia Parker asks: what gives an object significance? Parker utilizes the power of intervention, presentation, and transformation to imbue her sculptures, objects, and drawings with magical meaning. Her wide-ranging body of work includes her signature hanging sculptures, such as *Thirty Pieces of Silver* (1988-1989) made from hundreds of silver objects flattened by a steamroller, and *Cold Dark Matter: An Exploded View* (1991), created from the fragments of a shed exploded by the British Army. Many of Parker's works reference museum presentation, archiving, history, and the power of labeling, classification, and chance. Her conceptually and visually engaging oeuvre includes objects cut in half with the guillotine that killed Marie Antoinette, drawings made from the tarnish of objects once used by Davey Crockett and Charles Dickens, and a projection of dust and fibers from Sigmund Freud's couch. Her work speaks to the human fascination with collecting and studying those things associated with celebrity and history. Parker has had one-person shows at the Institute of Contemporary Art, Boston; the Serpentine Gallery, London; and ArtPace, San Antonio, Texas. In 1997, she was nominated for the Turner Prize, the prestigious award given annually to an outstanding British artist.

Barbara Steinman
Born 1950 in Montreal, Canada. Lives and works in Montreal, Canada.

Barbara Steinman's installations, video art, digital photography, and public sculpture mine the embedded stories of a given place. The visual beauty of Steinman's work draws viewers in, revealing many layers that address terror, injustice, and history. For *Signs* (1992), made for the Musée d'art contemporain de Montréal, Steinman installed sixty flashing signs similar in appearance to fire exit signs, which read "Silence." The work comments on Canada's language laws, as well as more general issues of censorship and control. Her sculpture, *Lux* (2000), consists of a chandelier of steel chains, suspended above a circle of crystals, as if the chandelier had shed its ornamentation like a tree in autumn. Steinman's work has been shown at the Museum of Modern Art, New York; the National Gallery of Canada, Ottawa; and the Jewish Museum, New York. It is in the collections of many museums including the Art Gallery of Ontario, Toronto, and the Seoul Metropolitan Museum in Korea. She is a recipient of the 2002 Governor General's Award in Canada, which recognizes outstanding lifetime achievement in the visual and media arts.

Mary Ellen Strom
Born 1957 in Butte, Montana. Lives and works in New York City.

Mary Ellen Strom is an interdisciplinary artist whose work has included video installation, performance, site-specific works, and public projects. Her art touches upon colonialism, politics, history, and surveillance. In 2000, she presented *GIRLS* at the High Museum in Atlanta, Georgia. This multimedia installation was created with and performed by a group of girls between the ages of 13 and 17, with whom Strom worked for over four years. Along with her individual projects, Strom often collaborates with performance artist/choreographer Ann Carlson. In 2003, the pair presented the video and performance installation *Geyser Land*. This unique project blended travel and tourism with art. Audiences experienced *Geyser Land* while riding a train between Livingston and Bozeman, Montana. *Geyser Land's* participants viewed video projections onto mountains, buildings, and industrial sites, and live performers recreating archival photographs through the train's windows. Strom's work has been exhibited internationally, including at the Museum of Contemporary Art, Los Angeles; the Museum of Modern Art, New York; the Museo de Arte, Mexico City; and Chapter Art Centre, Cardiff, Wales. She has received numerous awards including two New York Performance Awards for "Outstanding Creative Achievement." Strom was a 1999–2000 artist in the P.S.1/MoMA National Studio Program.

Nari Ward
Born 1963 in St. Andrews, Jamaica. Lives and works in New York City.

Nari Ward's work reveals his interest in decay, change, accumulation, consumerism, and history. He resuscitates found, discarded, or unwanted objects, including abandoned strollers, shopping carts, fire hoses, and mattresses. Ward gives these cast-offs new life, as well as a strange and enticing beauty, through his process of transforming them into sculpture. *Amazing Grace* (1993) consists of hundreds of baby strollers that Ward collected in Harlem and arranged in the shape of a ship's hull. For *Silent Mass Violent Whispers* (2001), a site-specific work in Trieste, Italy, Ward created a giant sphere from car mufflers and clothing. His work has been featured in many group exhibitions including Documenta XI in Kassel, Germany; the 1995 Whitney Biennial, New York; *The Quiet in the Land: Everyday Life, Contemporary Art, and the Shakers*, Institute of Contemporary Art, Maine College of Art, and the Institute of Contemporary Art, Boston; and *Crossing the Line*, Queens Museum of Art, New York. Ward has had solo exhibitions at the Isabella Stewart Gardner Museum, Boston; the Galleria Civica d'Arte Moderna e Contemporanea, Torino, Italy; and the New Museum of Contemporary Art, New York.

Krzysztof Wodiczko

Born 1943 in Warsaw, Poland. Lives and works in Cambridge, Massachusetts, and New York City.

Krzysztof Wodiczko is best known for creating large-scale public art works through projecting both still and moving images onto monuments and architecture. His projects are intimately linked to the politics, culture, history, and people of the cities in which he works. By using the built environment as the backdrop or "canvas" on which to stage his works, Wodiczko animates monuments and buildings, allowing them to speak of both past and present injustices. These deeply powerful, though fleeting, works present a space for dialogue and healing. Wodiczko has completed over seventy public projections around the world, including in his native Poland, Japan, Australia, Germany, Mexico, Ireland, Israel, and the United States. Wodiczko's essays on public art have been published in *October*, *Grand Street*, and *DIA Art Foundation's Discussion on Contemporary Culture*. In 1999, the MIT Press published *Critical Vehicles*, a collection of Wodiczko's writings, projects, and interviews. His work has been exhibited in numerous international art exhibitions including the Venice Biennale, the Lyon Biennale, and Documenta. He has had retrospective exhibitions at the Walker Art Center, Minneapolis; Fundacio Tapies, Barcelona; and the Wadsworth Atheneum, Hartford. In 1998, Wodiczko was awarded the Hiroshima Art Prize, which is given every three years to an artist whose work promotes peace.

The Institute of Contemporary Art is grateful to all of the following for their generous support, assistance and participation in ICA/Vita Brevis since its inception in 1998:

All of the commissioned artists; David Allakhverdov; American Express; American-Scandinavian Foundation; Anonymous; Barco U.S.A., Harriet Barlow; Colby Berger; Denise Bergman; Rebecca Blunk; BMValla, Reykjavik; Bosport Docking; Boston Conservation Commission; Boston Courthouse Management Associates; Boston Cultural Agenda Fund; Boston Cultural Council; Boston Fire Department, Engine 33; the Boston Foundation; Boston Foundation for Architecture; Boston Landmarks Commission; Boston National Historical Park/National Park Service; Boston Parks and Recreation Department; Boston Police Archives; Debra Browder; Bunker Hill Monument Association; Capron Lighting and Sound; Stacey Carson; Sage Carter; Sarah Chapman; Charlestown After Murder Program and Sandy King, Pam Enos, Terry Titcomb; Charlestown Neighborhood Council; Chase Manhattan Foundation; Children's Hospital Boston, Center on Media and Child Health; CIMS; Citizen's Bank; Susan Courtemanche; Weldon Covey; Danish American Contemporary Art Foundation; Sally DeAngelis; Kelley Donovan; Eleanor Duckworth; EIMSKIP; the Emerald Necklace Conservancy; Jonathan Evans; Paul and Phyllis Fireman Charitable Foundation; First Night, Inc.; Darren Foote; Herb Fox; the Freedom Trail Foundation; Sarah Freeman; Fund for the Arts/New England Foundation for the Arts; Goethe-Institut, Boston; Daniel and Sarah Goldhagen; Daniel Gonzalez; Marian Goodman Gallery; Greater Boston Arts, WGBH; the Gunk Foundation; Julia Gunn, R.N.; Lt. Eric Hahn, Harbormaster, Boston Police Department; William Heddon, Fox Hill Studios; Joan Heminway; Hercules Steel; Manna Hesch, R.N.; Nedda Hobbs; Helen Hoerman; Michael Hoerman; Steven Hubbard, The Planning Stage; Joseph Hudson and Catherine Hillenbrand; Todd Jick and Rose Zoltek-Jick; the Kapor Family Foundation; Kristen Kissik; Steven Kozlowski; Dr. Andrew Kurban; Barbara Lee; LEF Foundation; Liz Lerman; Michael Patrick MacDonald; Gregory Maguire; Denise Markonish; Elizabeth Marks and Paul Taylor; Iris Martinez; Massachusetts Convention Center Authority, Massachusetts Cultural Council; Massachusetts Foundation for the Humanities; Massachusetts State Archives; Mayor's Office of Cultural Affairs, Boston; James Earl McCoy; Madeline McNeely; Leon and Phyllis Medvedow; Andrew W. Mellon Foundation; Metropolitan District Commission; Monument Square Association; Sylvia Morrison; James Nadeau; National Dance Project/New England Foundation for the Arts; National Endowment for the Arts; Neighborhood Association of the Back Bay; Neptune Marine Services; Peter Norton Family Foundation; Joan Norris; Greg and Heather Oaksen; Office of the Boston Police Commissioner; Old North Church; Old South Meeting House; Sophie Parker; Dillon Paul; Diana Perry; Phillip Morris Companies; Wanda Phipatanakul, M.D.; Lia and William Poorvu; Preston Productions; Pure and Simply Gourmet; Michael Rich, M.D.; Karen Rosen; Mitch Rosenberg; Elizabeth Saari; Lisa Schmidt; School of the Museum of Fine Arts; Anne Schwartz; Morgan Schwartz; Sea Chain; Liz Sevcenko; Michael Shannon, M.D.; Noel Day Sidford; Skanska; Society for the Preservation of New England Antiquities; Sonesta Charitable Foundation; Jeanne and Donald Stanton; Sterling Equipment; Surdna Foundation; Susan Taylor; Denise Thal and David Scobey; Jennifer Tipton; Bernard Toale and Joe Zina; Nanette Tobin and Rick Vallely; Ina and Philip Trager; Emily Hall Tremaine Exhibition Award; Volunteer Lawyers for the Arts, Boston Chapter; Wallace-Readers Digest Fund; Katherine Chandler Wallace; Andy Warhol Foundation for the Visual Arts; WBZ-TV4; the Weekly TAB; Lauren Weinger; Lorraine Wild; SGT Williams, USAR, 309th Combat Support Hospital.

Vita Brevis: *History, Landscape, and Art 1998-2003* has received generous support from the Elizabeth Firestone Graham Foundation.

Institute of Contemporary Art Staff

Jill Medvedow, James Sachs Plaut Director
Nicholas Baume, Chief Curator
Paul Bessire, Director of External Relations
Mary Blank, Accountant
Branka Bogdanov, Film, Video & Performance Producer
Jamie Davis, Foundation and Government Relations Officer
Karen DeTemple, Individual Support Manager
Nora Donnelly, Registrar
Joe Douillette, Fast Forward Coordinator
Brigham Fay, Assistant to the Director
Sara Farragher, Development Operations and Research Coordinator
Ena Fox, Director of Education
Jeremy Grainger, Bookstore Manager
Svanhildur Karadottir, Gallery Manager
Melissa Kuronen, Communications Manager
June Mattioli, Special Events Manager
Sandi Clement McKinley,
Associate Director of Development, Major Gifts
Carole Anne Meehan, ICA/Vita Brevis Project Director
Chris Mekal, Project Director for the New ICA
Emily Moore, Curatorial Assistant
Svetlana Murguz, Administrative Assistant
Tim Obetz, Exhibitions/Facilities Manager
Lizzi Ross, Public Programs Manager
Janna Schultz, Corporate, Foundation, and Government Relations Manager
Amanda Silberman, Assistant Gallery Manager
Bennett Simpson, Associate Curator
Michael Taubenberger, Director of Finance and Operations
Tiffanie Ting, Education Assistant
Christina Watson, Membership and Annual Giving Coordinator

Photography credits
Shimon Attie
James Boorstein
David Carmack
Phillip Jones
Kennedy + Violich
Suara Welitoff
National Park Service

First edition 2004

Book design: Steidl Design / Claas Möller
Scans done at Steidl's digital darkroom
Production and printing: Steidl, Göttingen

Steidl
Düstere Str. 4 / D-37073 Göttingen
Phone +49 551-49 60 60 / Fax +49 551-49 60 649
E-mail: mail@steidl.de / www.steidl.de

ISBN 3-88243-816-9
Printed in Germany